SARAWAK
Kapuas
Mahu
BORNEO
Barito
Manggar
Balikpapan
STRAIT OF MACASS
Bandjermasin
Oelin
Tg. Puting
Tg. Selatan
Laoet Is.
Laoet K! Is
Keramian I.
Masalima I.
Kalu Kalukuang
Macassar
EA
Salembau I.
Bawean I.
One Macassar Prahu Course East
Kangean Is.
MADOERA
Soerabaia
Madioen
Malang
Pasirian
3 Sailing Ships Course S. E.
Singaradja
BALI
LOMBOK
Den Pasar
Tafelhoek
P. Nusa Besar
Lombok Str.
Selong
SOEMBAWA
Powerful Searchlight sighted from this area
OCEAN
The Course of the KRAIT
Miles
0
50
100
150
200
2
0
2
4
6
8
10
112
114
116
118
120

RETURN OF THE TIGER

By the same author

MANIFEST DESTINY
KNIGHT ERRANT
A WATCHER ON THE RHINE
PORTRAIT OF A GOLDEN AGE
THE SAVAGE YEARS

In collaboration with Putzi Hanfstaengl

UNHEARD WITNESS

In collaboration with John, Duke of Bedford

A SILVER-PLATED SPOON

Edited and translated in collaboration

MEMOIRS: FRANZ VON PAPEN
THE BOMBARD STORY, Alain Bombard

In preparation

THE PALMERSTON PAPERS 1.
The correspondence between Queen Victoria and Viscount Palmerston 1837–1865

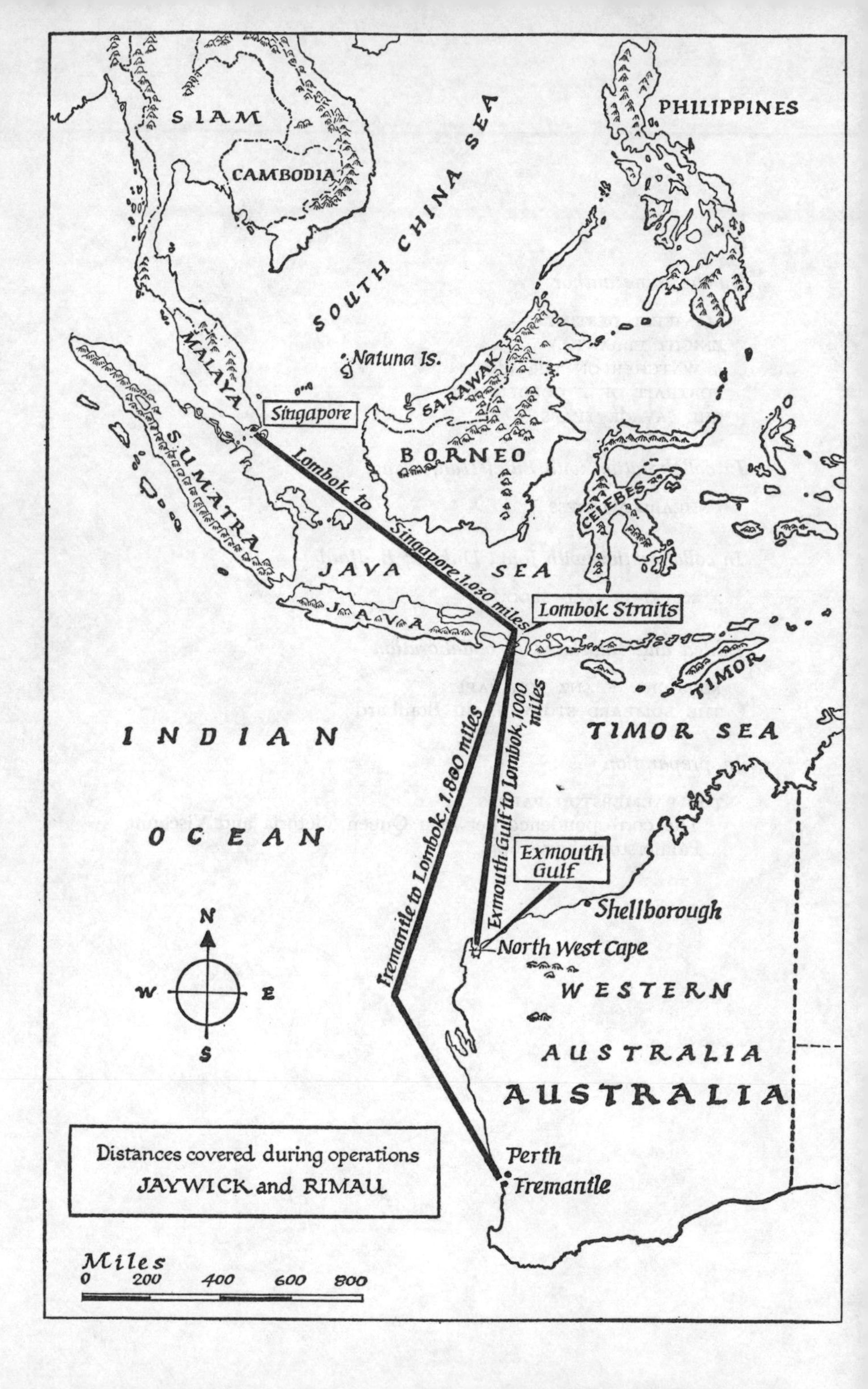
SIAM
CAMBODIA
SOUTH CHINA SEA
PHILIPPINES
MALAYA
Natuna Is.
SARAWAK
Singapore
SUMATRA
BORNEO
Lombok to Singapore, 1,030 miles
CELEBES
JAVA SEA
JAVA
Lombok Straits
TIMOR
TIMOR SEA
INDIAN
OCEAN
Fremantle to Lombok, 1,800 miles
Exmouth Gulf to Lombok, 1000 miles
Exmouth Gulf
Shellborough
North West Cape
N
W
E
S
WESTERN
AUSTRALIA
AUSTRALIA
Distances covered during operations
JAYWICK and RIMAU
Perth
Fremantle
Miles
0 200 400 600 800

RETURN OF THE TIGER

Doubleday & Company, Inc., Garden City, New York,

BY BRIAN CONNELL

PRINTED IN THE UNITED STATES OF AMERICA

DESIGN: CHARLES KAPLAN

To ESMÉE,
for whom my return has meant only hard labour.

CONTENTS

In peace there's nothing so becomes a man
As modest stillness and humility;
But when the blast of war blows in our ears,
Then imitate the action of the tiger;
Stiffen the sinews, summon up the blood,
Disguise fair nature with hard-favour'd rage;
Then lend the eye a terrible aspect.

Henry V III, i
William Shakespeare

FOREWORD

THE BRITISH MIDGET-SUBMARINE ATTACK ON THE *Tirpitz*, the Italian human-torpedo raids on Gibraltar and Alexandria, and the Japanese penetration of Sydney Harbour rank as some of the most spectacular irregular raids of the last war. Yet here is a story surpassing them all in courage and daring, exceeding each in the distance covered and difficulties surmounted, which seems completely to have escaped general notice. In the autumn of 1943 and 1944, canoe teams, armed with limpet mines, were carried in rickety native motorboat and junk thousands of miles across enemy waters from Australia to attack Japanese convoys in Singapore Roads. Some 40,000 tons of merchant shipping were sunk. Both expeditions were conceived and led by the same man, yet apart from a few initiates, no one seems to have heard of them.

I was myself captured by the Japanese in Indochina on Pearl Harbor Day. After my return to England, I was attached to a Royal Marine Commando during the North European Campaign, and although I was fairly conversant with some of the odder aspects of war, these raids on Singapore had never come to my notice. If they were romanticised or written as fiction I doubt if anyone would believe them to be based on fact. For someone of my generation, which had seven years taken out of its useful life by the war, both enthusiasm and homage demand that this astonishing story be rescued from oblivion. Every line of this book is based on documentary records and eye-witness accounts.

If A. J. A. Symons had not already written *The Quest for Corvo*, I could have fashioned this book as a description of the research work involved. It began eighteen months ago, when an acquaintance said to me at a cocktail party one evening, "Why don't you write up the story of Ivan Lyon?" I have to confess that I answered: "Who on earth was he?" My informant knew the bare outlines of Lyon's exploits and had at one time been an intimate of his family, although he had lost their address.

Lyon had been a regular in the Gordon Highlanders, so my first letter went to the barracks at Bridge of Don. He had led his raids while seconded for special duties, and although they had at one time held a few press cuttings in their records, these had been mislaid. His father, formerly a brigadier in the Royal Artillery, was dead, and they had no address for his next of kin. There was nothing of consequence in the Admiralty or War Office records, and a few scattered Australian press cuttings dated 1945 and 1946 whetted the appetite without adding greatly to the information.

My attention was then drawn to a book written by the widow of the second-in-command of Lyon's expeditions, entitled *Winning Hazard*, under the pen name of Noel Wynyard. It had long since been out of print and seems to have attracted very little notice. I managed to obtain a second-hand copy and found that it dealt only with the first expedition. However, it did contain a full list of its fourteen members, most of whom were Australians. To reconstruct the complete story from the original sources, I therefore turned to the Commonwealth Navy Board in Canberra, who have been the soul of helpfulness throughout. They undertook to forward letters to the few known survivors, but not one elicited a reply, although I scoured Australia with advertisements in the ex-servicemen's magazines.

I was about to abandon the entire project when a last desperate telephone call turned the tide. Permission had recently been given for bona fide enquirers to obtain information about the activities during the war of the Special Operations Executive. I had no reason to suppose that Lyon's expeditions had been organised under the auspices of S.O.E., but to my delight, they were, and all my requests for information were most fully and courteously answered. For this I owe a special debt of gratitude to Lieutenant-Colonel E. G. Boxshall, M.B.E., of the Foreign Office, who has at all times gone out of his way to render me the utmost cooperation and assistance. I was also able to contact Lieutenant-Colonel W. W. Chapman, still commanding a territorial battalion of Royal Engineers, who had devised most of the equipment for the second expedition, had accompanied them on the outward trip, and had then led the pick-up party into the South China seas.

Although I had by now amassed plenty of documentary evidence, I still needed to find at least one eye-witness of the first expedition. I tracked him down at last in the person of Warrant Officer R. G. Morris, R.A.M.C., still in the service, back in England, at Tidworth. It had taken me a year to find him. Both he and Colonel Chapman are blessed with lively descriptive minds and happily retentive memories and are largely responsible for making this reconstruction of two incredible adventures possible.

Many of the quotations in the final chapter from captured Japanese records coincide with those in an article entitled "Expedition to Singkep," in *Blackwood's Magazine* of October 1946, by Major Cyril Wild, who was an interpreter on the Allied War Crimes Commission in Singapore. Towards the end of my research work, I found cursory and somewhat inaccurate accounts outlining Lyon's exploits in two American books dealing with larger aspects of the Pacific war: *Spy Ring Pacific*, by Allison Ind, and *MacArthur: 1941–51*, by Major-General C. A. Willoughby and John Chamberlain.

The Australian Commonwealth Navy Board also most generously placed at my disposal a photocopy of the invaluable navigator's log of the first expedition kept by Lieutenant H. C. Carse, R.A.N.V.R. I have in addition been able to quote from the official reports of Lieutenant-Colonel Ivan Lyon, Lieutenant-Commander D. Davidson, R.N.V.R., Lieutenant-Colonel W. W. Chapman, R.E. My best thanks go to Lieutenant-Colonel R. G. Lees, Gordon Highlanders, who served with Lyon in Malaya prior to the outbreak of war, and Mrs. Lees, Captain D. Fogg-Elliot at the Gordon Highlanders Museum, Bridge of Don, Lieutenant-Colonel P. St. C. Harrison, Regimental Secretary of the King's Own Scottish Borderers, James Dowdall, the Lyon family friend who started it all, and, particularly, to Mrs. Ann Gordon, née Lyon, whose fond memories of her brother have brought his whole personality to life. I am also most grateful to his widowed mother, Mrs. Frank Lyon, for allowing me to read his private letters and other family documents. My wife and I have been greatly relieved of many routine typing chores by Miss Gillian Foote and Miss Barbara Barnes.

I have found it necessary to use a few Malay words in their context, and although their meaning is fairly obvious, these translations may prove useful:

Atap palm foliage used for building native huts
Kampong a village or fishing settlement
Kolek a native canoe
Pagar a complex of fixed fishing nets surrounding a moored houseboat
Parang a bush-knife of the machete type
Prahu a native sailing craft of the junk type
Pulau also variously *puloe, pulo, pulai*—an island
Rimau the Malay word for tiger
Sampan a small native dinghy

Sarong	a cylinder of cotton cloth doubled back round the waist and rolled over at the top—a standard item of native clothing
Tanjong	a cape or point of land

London
1st October 1960

RETURN OF THE TIGER

1

IVAN LYON

CHAOS WAS CLOSING IN ON SINGAPORE DURING THE LAST January days of 1942. Over the causeway from Johore Bahru had come stumbling the beaten British Army in Malaya, outflanked, outthought, outfought, outgeneralled and demoralised. The fortress without defences, an area about the size of the Isle of Wight, with its big naval guns pointing out into the South China Sea, was teeming with 100,000 troops. Scattered round the 72-mile perimeter in isolated units, guarding every point but concentrating on none, their chains of command disorganised, the reinforcements which had come by sea untrained, looking over their shoulders at snipers, fifth columnists, and the escape route through the port, they waited for their collective neck to be wrung. The worst surrender in British military history was in the making.

Every day, over their dumps, their airfields, their headquarters, the city, and the port, relays of Japanese bombers in perfect V-formation dropped their hourly cargo. In between, dive-bombers screamed down with their anti-personnel grasscutters, showering razor-sharp shrapnel on soldier and civilian alike. Zero fighters roared at treetop level along the roads, spraying staff cars and rickshaws, even the milkman on his rounds, with searing bullets. Then the guns on the mainland opened up, their targets long since pinpointed by the network of spies carefully planted in the years that had led up to Pearl Harbor Day. The remaining British artillery opened up too, firing blind into the bush to the north, while the few naval guns which could be swung round sent their armour-piercing shells arcing over the island into nowhere. It was like trying to kill a mosquito with a rifle bullet.

The green island, suspended from the southern tip of Asia in the brilliant blue sea, like an emerald brooch displayed on azure velvet, shook under the crump of the shells and detonations. The clear sky of the tropical spring was never free of the smoke haze that came from the leaping fires of burning warehouse and ignited petrol dump. As the fatal fifteen days of February dawned, men's minds switched from the desperate conjecture of how they could still fight on, to the nagging thought of how to get away.

There were now no less than five senior army headquarters concentrated in this growing inferno: the Malayan Command of General Percival at Fort Canning, the futile "Battle Box," General Simmond's Fortress Command, General Heath's 3rd Indian Corps, General Beckwith-Smith's 18th British Division, which had only just arrived after spending three months cooped up on the high seas, and the Australian Imperial Force Command of General Gordon Bennett.

"Piggy" Heath, commander of the 3rd Corps, a better general than the mutiny of his Hyderabads and the useless quality of the recruits supplied by an over-expanded Indian Army would indicate, had his head-quarters in a hutted camp in the north-eastern sector of the island. There, shortly after they had settled in, his morning conference was interrupted by an immediate air-raid warning. The staff officers who still graced the Raffles Hotel every evening ducked out into the slit trenches for cover. Also present was Major Lees of the Gordon Highlanders, one of the few units to have maintained its coherence and dignity throughout this sorry campaign. He half rose to follow the rest, assuming that this was the normal drill, when he saw that the general had remained in his seat. So had a young captain, who had left the regiment a couple of months earlier to volunteer for special duties, named Ivan Lyon.

Lees knew him well although he had not seen him for some time, as the regiment had been up-country and had only just returned to take up position in the shaky defences. Lyon, as usual, was puffing away at an enormous pipe in clouds of smoke. So was the general, who wanted to hear from the young captain details of the "stay-behind" parties which Lyon was helping to organise to harry the Japanese lines of communication down the Malayan peninsula. With the bombers roaring overhead and the bombs thudding, Lees took out his own pipe, muttering to himself that he was damned if he was going out into any slit trench as long as a young captain from his own regiment did not do so, and stayed until it was over.

The secret organisation Lyon had joined was known as Force 136, housed in the tall Cathay Building on Singapore's waterfront. It was part of the world-wide network of saboteurs and spies being built up by the Special Operations Executive with headquarters in London's Baker Street. Under its dynamic local commander, Colonel Alan Warren of the Royal Marines, it was one of the few branches of the services desperately trying to do something positive among the military wreckage crashing all round it.

The fate of Singapore had been sealed long before the Japanese invaded Malaya. Stereotyped military thinking and a total inability to foresee the sort of war the Japanese would wage crippled the British Army and high command from the start. First, and erroneously, it was believed, at the urgent promptings of the British ambassador in Bangkok, that the Siamese would stand firm and prevent the Japanese surging across from Indochina, where they had been stationed since the fall of France. Then it was assumed that enemy troop convoys crossing the Gulf of Siam would be sunk either by the Royal Navy or the R.A.F. and that any remnants would be safely mopped up as they came ashore. Thirdly, and disastrously, it was taken for granted that the Japanese could only advance down the main highways and railways which served the British Army in Malaya as its comfortable lines of communication.

All this proved false. Siam folded up overnight, the

Royal Navy was crippled by the loss of the *Prince of Wales* and the *Repulse*, the R.A.F. was blown out of the air by the faster and more manoeuvrable Zero fighters, and the Japanese Army advanced through mangrove swamps and paddy fields, skirting fixed defences, which were abandoned as soon as they had been by-passed. No real attempt had been made by the British to mobilise the local population, no preparations had been made for field defence positions, and there was no mobile reserve.

One of the best features of the British Army is its ability to produce unorthodox warriors, and one of its worst is its inability to appreciate or use them in time. A few clear heads had foreseen the threat of jungle warfare and had tried to devise means of beating the Japanese on their own ground. The idea of organising scores of self-contained sabotage parties to harass the enemy and report on their movements should war begin and the invasion forces break through the inadequately held defences of northern Malaya, had been mooted months back. It had always been turned down by the Governor, Sir Shenton Thomas, and general headquarters on the grounds that such a plan, if put into operation, would have a disastrous psychological effect on the Malayan population. To put arms in the hands of the Chinese, who formed nearly half the inhabitants and most of whom were regarded as potential Communists, verged on the treasonable.

Those more farsighted fought vainly to overcome official obstructionism. One of these was Colonel John

Dalley, director of the intelligence bureau of the Malayan Security Police. He had a nucleus of three to four thousand Malays and Chinese who would be ideal for the purpose, but for the time being he was forbidden to make more out of them than a sort of local Home Guard.

Almost in defiance of authority, another organisation, called No. 101 Special Training School, had been formed in a millionaire's villa on an island off Singapore at which intelligent young Chinese were trained to operate behind enemy lines as wireless operators and saboteurs. The instructors included such famous names as Jim Gavin, who had set up the first commando training school at Lochailort on the west coast of Scotland, with "Mad Mike" Calvert, subsequently a Wingate brigadier, and also Freddie Spencer-Chapman, whose best-selling post-war book *The Jungle Is Neutral* was to tell the fantastic story of those who did succeed in staying behind in Malaya. Ivan Lyon was another such, whose subsequent exploits in the South China seas matched theirs for sheer daring and incredibility.

Tall, slim, not particularly robust, with a quick, urgent walk, Ivan Lyon had the sort of face at which you looked twice. The brown skin was stretched tightly over the high cheekbones and his thick chestnut hair curled becomingly over his small, hard head. But the most striking feature was his eyes, curiously elongated, almost oriental but for the startling sea-green of their irises. Eyes that could flash the colour of emeralds in his rare bursts of anger or contempt. The little military moustache was almost an unnecessary appendage. Clean-shaven, in the dark of a sabotage raid, he might even have passed for a Malay.

The only incongruous feature was a slightly tip-tilted nose, liable to skin in the hot sun. Normally reserved, even taciturn, except in the presence of close friends and family, he would occasionally break into an enchanting smile which revealed a great flash of superb teeth. He believed that no gentleman should laugh immoderately and he had one of the longest family trees in all Scotland.

The Lyons trace themselves back with pride to the thirteenth century. They are cousins of the Bowes-Lyons, and, like all his immediate family, Ivan had the right to wear the Royal Stuart tartan. His forebears for generations before him had been regular soldiers. His father had been at the siege of Ladysmith, fought with extreme gallantry on the Somme, and had ended his career as a military attaché in the Balkans and Brussels. The first son had been delicate, and Ivan, although the third of five children, became the natural leader of his elder sister and younger brother and sister.

Even as a boy, he was the adventurous type, and although devoted to his family, curiously solitary. At home, in the summer, he loathed being cooped up in his room, and preferred to sleep out on the roof, under an umbrella if necessary. The Lyons spent long winter holidays in the Tyrol, where he became an expert skier, never happier than when touring, often dangerously, in the deep snow by himself. Sailing was another passion, and his first choice of a profession was the Navy. He failed the entrance examination into Dartmouth although his greatest boyhood friend, who only wanted to join to stay with Ivan, got in. They joined forces again later to make a long canoe trip down the Danube.

By then, Ivan was at Harrow, where his housemaster, Mr. Gannon, used to take a few boys on summer sailing trips during the vacation. Ivan became an adept and, at the age of seventeen, won a trophy for taking a sailing canoe across to Denmark single-handed. He was already the lone-wolf type in his teens, and a school friend remembers catching a glimpse of him leaning on a gate out in the paddock at the family home near Farnham, whittling away at a stick and happily absorbed in his own thoughts.

Family tradition was still strong enough for him to go to Sandhurst. Then he joined the Gordon Highlanders, the first of the Lyons to do so. All the others had been Gunners. He never really took to regimental life, and loathed garrison duties most of all. He used to regale his favourite older sister, Ann Gordon, married to an Australian naval officer, with scarifying tales of the monstrous troop of mothers who prowled into the mess on gala days looking for eligible husbands for their daughters, most of whom, he was convinced, wore thick Harris-tweed nightdresses. Ivan Lyon was no ascetic. He was extremely attractive to women, with his brooding good looks, but beneath his reserved air he had a distinctly impish sense of humour. One year, knowing the delight these mothers took in receiving regimental Christmas cards, he went out and bought a batch illustrated with cats and sent them off.

Not that military life embittered him. At home, his family found him the same unruffled, quietly humourous Ivan. Many an evening he would sit silently by the fire with a glass of beer, puffing away at the enormous pipe which had become his trademark and reading voraciously. As long as he was lost in another world he seemed completely happy. If there was some household upset or flurry, he would look up and say: "Now then, ladies, no panic," and all the difficulties would be ironed out.

Then, at the beginning of 1937, his battalion was sent out to Malaya. Garrison life in pre-war Singapore did little to change his habits. Apart from the Leeses and Willy Graham, the colonel, who divined his true quality, he had few friends. He was always the lone wolf. He did his regimental duties as a subaltern well, even devising new methods of training for his platoon to break the boredom, but he never really mixed with his fellow officers or adopted their cliché-ridden military jargon. He read a lot, puffed away at his inseparable pipe, and his mind was always elsewhere. No one really knew where. At that time he probably did not know himself. What he was subconsciously seeking was action, if possible independent action, and his senior officers realised that he would never stay with the regiment permanently. He was the type to volunteer for a Himalayan expedition, service with a special force operating to put down some local uprising, or anything to get away from the routine that oppressed him.

His one real interest remained sailing. Soon after his arrival in Singapore, he succeeded in acquiring a sturdy, three-ton, ocean-going yawl called the *Vinette*. With another officer in the regiment named Francis Moir Byres, he started exploring the nearby islands of the Rhio Archipelago and then ventured on longer trips up the eastern coast of Malaya as far as Siam. He found he could expose himself without discomfort to the tropical sun, wearing only a singlet and a damp cloth round his neck. He would often put in at native fishing villages for the night and he quickly acquired an excellent working knowledge of Malay.

Sailing so engrossed him that he saved up his local leave for the purpose of making longer trips. At the end of his first year in garrison, he leapt at the opportunity to crew a 12-ton Australian yacht, the *Kewarra*, on a cruise through the then Dutch East Indies to Darwin. The owner, J. A. Gagan, was a gifted navigator, and by the time Lyon returned on a freighter he had become an expert with chart, sextant, and tide-tables himself.

The regiment tried to appease his wanderlust by allowing him to take his company on jungle manoeuvres up-country. His letters home described how he was teaching them to navigate through the jungle using nautical methods, cooking their own food, and learning to live with the local population. What his men thought of the experiments is not recorded, but the interlude provides a fascinating forerunner of the tactics developed by Wingate in Burma and "Mike" Calvert in the post-war S.A.S. Regiment. Lyon was an innovator, but he had yet to find an outlet for his fertile mind.

Back in barracks, depression set in again. The other officers annoyed him with their endless, empty chatter, and he complained that he was lucky to find enough work to keep him occupied for an hour a day. He was also very hard up. *Vinette* was a big drain on his modest pocket and the accounting system of the mess swallowed up the rest of his pay. The cost of entertaining guests—mostly planters, for whose company Lyon had even less time—was divided up according to rank among all the officers. Although Lyon seldom attended these routs, he still had to pay his share, and this infuriated him.

Restlessly, he cast around for some escape. He thought of joining the Malay Regiment, which would at least bring him in contact with the true inhabitants, but this his father vetoed. Then he announced his intention of resigning from the regiment and sailing round the world in *Vinette*. Even if his family cut off his modest allowance, an Australian girl friend had offered to help finance the trip. He felt he could not stand the drudgery of an infantry regiment any longer, standing around for hours slapping his swagger stick against his thigh.

Somehow this crisis was smoothed over. Perhaps as a gesture of defiance, as ostentation was not in his nature, he had gone one day to a native tattooist in Singapore and had a tremendous tiger's head imprinted on his chest. It cost him three hours of agony, and the revolting, leering beast, in black and yellow, with staring red eyes, stretched almost from his navel to his collarbones. It certainly made him an even greater oddity in the regiment, although it was widely admired and Willy Graham once made him take off his shirt in the anteroom to exhibit it. It was a curious fancy, which he explained in due course to his sister by saying that once he had made up his mind to have a tattoo of some sort, there was not much point in the usual heart and arrow, with the legend "I love Mary," as he would always have to be changing the inscription. In fact, another name was about to qualify for permanent inclusion.

It was on another lone sailing trip, this time to Saigon, that he met his wife. Running into a severe storm not far from the French penal settlement of Pulau Condore, *Vinette*'s sails were so damaged that he had to put in for repairs. The French Governor gave him every assistance and introduced Ivan Lyon to his daughter Gabrielle, a petite, lively, lovely girl who had been married at the age of sixteen, but was divorced, with a young daughter. By the time Lyon left, they were hopelessly in love. They were married in Saigon on July 27, 1939.

They found an attractive bungalow out in the wooded country near Singapore, and Gabrielle was a superb cook. The regimental mess saw even less of Lyon than before, although he and Gabrielle became frequent visitors to the Leeses and the Grahams. Three months before war broke out in the Far East, they had a son, Clive, to whom Mrs. Graham stood godmother.

In the meantime, Lyon had found some respite from his regimental duties. He was seconded for intelligence work, although he was still pulled back from time to time to the Gordon Highlanders. When France fell, and General Catroux, the Governor-General of Indochina, left to join the Free French forces, Lyon was attached to him as aide-de-camp, guide, and interpreter. Thereafter he functioned as a liaison officer with the Free French as a G.S.O. III on the staff of Sir Geoffrey Layton, the naval C.-in-C. of the China Station. While Gaby supplemented their income broadcasting to Indochina, Lyon travelled extensively round the Far East on his duties, and he was in Batavia when their son was born.

He hurried back, only to find that there was a new requirement for his services. The advocates of irregular warfare in the event of a Japanese invasion were at last starting to get a hearing, and they had marked down Lyon as a promising recruit. The war clouds were gathering now and the Gordons also wanted him back. He had grown out of the routine of regimental exercises, parades, and ceremonial. To his imaginative mind, they seemed poor preparation for the coming conflict. The thin red line was no longer going to serve the needs of modern war. When opportunity arose to volunteer blind for special duties with the embryo Force 136, he leapt at the chance. The Gordons had lost a good subaltern, but the Army had gained a recruit to the small band to which its Wingates, Stirlings, and Calverts belong.

With Singapore becoming untenable, Lyon saw Gabrielle and his little son off on one of the transports which had brought in the ill-fated 18th Division and sailed again with thousands of wives and families from the beleaguered city for Australia and safety. Lyon was preparing to go up-country with the guerrillas when Colonel Warren sent for him.

"Things are going badly, Ivan," he said. "You know the islands south of Singapore. We must try and keep the lines open through Sumatra even if we are overrun here. If the worst comes to the worst, we may get part of the army out and whatever happens we shall want to get people in again. It means food dumps, buttering up the natives, and setting up local resistance groups if we can. I am sending out John Davis, Richard Broome, and Jock Campbell, and I want you to go with them."

Davis and Broome, in due course, were to rejoin Freddie Spencer-Chapman in the Malayan jungles. "Jock" Campbell was a recent recruit to the organisation. A successful planter and well-known *bon viveur*, he had been general manager of the Socfin Plantations up in Selangor State and, when that was overrun, made his way back to Singapore, where, late in December, he had quickly been commissioned as a major in the General List, and, from peace-time connection with the regiment back in Scotland as a territorial, wore the uniform of the King's Own Scottish Borderers.

Lyon was not too pleased at the assignment. He had seen too many army deserters and faint-hearted Singapore businessmen prowling the docks seeking some avenue of escape. He did not want it to look as if he was going the same way, but Colonel Warren was insistent. "Very well, sir," said Lyon, "but if I go that way now I'll make damn sure to be one of the first back."

Lyon, who always had a sharp eye for likely, self-reliant men among the troops, had taken approving note of the medical orderly at 101 S.T.S., a lively Welsh ex-coal miner who, by sheer dogged persistence, had passed his exams in the R.A.M.C. and had been seconded for duty at the Sabotage Training School. Quick, sturdy, cheerful, and reliable, "Taffy" Morris was very much a jack-of-all-trades, with a steady look in his intelligent eyes and a reassuring firmness behind the Rhondda lilt of his voice. He too was bored with his job and more than a little envious of the trainees he had seen being sent up-country. When Lyon asked him if he would like to accompany the party to the south, he leapt at the opportunity, requisitioned a Sten gun out of the armoury, although it was contrary to all regulations for a medical corpsman to carry a weapon, and gleefully went out to practise on the rifle range.

Singapore was entering the fever of its final days. At the Adelphi Hotel, Reller's Band was still playing Palm Court selections; there were endless queues for the cinemas; the Raffles Hotel and the officers' clubs were packed with the myriad staff officers who had discovered no other method of spending their off-duty time. 101 S.T.S. was being rapidly disbanded and the personnel dispersed about their duties before the Japanese could capture the unit entire and discover all their secrets. Morris was housed for a couple of days at the Union Jack Club while final preparations for the dash south were made and then, at short notice, joined Lyon, Campbell, and the others on a little Malayan steamer with a Chinese crew moored at Clifford Pier.

As they cast off, the doomed island shook under its smoke haze from the incessant bombardment that heralded its death throes. They steamed south to the Tjombol Straits, which separate Sumatra and the off-shore islands from those of the Rhio Archipelago. Astern, the dancing lights of the innumerable fires slowly twinkled below the horizon, leaving a garish glow in the night sky. Deprived of his pipe by the black-out, Lyon stood at the stern-rail, brooding. If Singapore fell, some way would have to be found of getting back, to harass an enemy about to overrun the whole of Asia.

Morris soon proved his worth. There were quite a number of injured passengers, and after he had splinted them up or adjusted their dressings where necessary, he started poking round in the little ship, found a few carrots and potatoes and an odd, unidentified tin of meat, and in no time had a three-gallon cauldron brewing over a charcoal fire so that everyone could have a bowl of hot stew. Lyon had chosen well.

The escape route had already been roughly plotted. The main trans-shipment point was to be the island of Pulau Durian off the coast of Sumatra. The pipeline then led up the estuary of the Indragiri River from Pridiraja to Rengat, the highest navigable point, and thence over the road through the hills to Padang on the west coast, where the Royal Navy was concentrating what ships it could to take them on to Ceylon and India. Jock Campbell took charge at Rengat, while Lyon and Morris were left on Pulau Durian, where a food dump had been deposited. They built themselves an *atap* hut on the top of the 200-foot hill overlooking the tiny harbour and waited for the worst.

While they were preparing for survivors to flood through the pipe-line, Morris was able to study the slim, young captain who had pulled him out of his sick bay and now had him on the top of a jungle island soon to be surrounded by a sea of Japanese. Quiet, friendly, doing his full share of their joint chores, he would spend most of his day sitting away on a tree stump, sucking at his inevitable pipe. Tobacco was the one form of personal stores he had equipped himself with richly. Morris soon acquired the same impression Lyon had given to the officers of his regiment. He was never quite with his companions, but appeared to be mulling some plan or enterprise over in his mind. His attention was miles away. At this time he did not yet confide in Morris, but the day would come when he would tell the corporal how his thoughts were running.

It was not long before the refugees began streaming southward, and as Singapore's surrender day of February 15 arrived, the trickle became a flood. There were those who had escaped, those who had been ordered to go for various reasons—nursing sisters, soldiers, civilians, Malays, Chinese, wives, and children. Those who arrived direct were fairly easy to pass through, but Japanese aircraft and naval patrol vessels were starting to scour the islands and the evacuation became a desperate game of hide-and-seek.

The worst episode, which had Lyon and Morris working eighty hours at a stretch, came with the bombing off Pompong Island, to the east, of three ships which had left Singapore for Batavia, the *Kuala*, *Tunkuang*, and *Kuangwo,* Chinese river steamers and gunboats pressed into service for the purpose just as Singapore was falling.

As they were passing Pompong Island, at the inward end of the Temiang Strait, between the Rhio and the Lingga groups of islands, the Japanese bombers struck. All three were set on fire and sunk, but nearly 700 survivors, many of the women in nightdresses, the men in what they had stripped to for the swim, succeeded in reaching the shore. Apart from a few fishing shacks, Pompong was uninhabited. The survivors had no food, only such water as the island supplied and no shelter. Huddled in the jungle in their hundreds, many died, so that the natives ever after called it the Island of Ghosts, but Lyon's organisation saved the vast majority.

In this they were helped by the fanatically loyal Malay Amir Silalahi of Senajang, who, from Singkep Island to the south, mobilised every villager's junk, moved in such food as he had at his disposal, and, with the help of the other launches and small craft of the escape organisation, ferried them all over to Pulau Durian, where they were passed on to Campbell at Rengat and safety.

It was during this hectic period that Lyon met a grizzled, blasphemous, elderly Australian named Bill

Reynolds, who had brought a load of refugees out of Singapore in a decrepit seventy-foot-long coaster with an ancient diesel engine. Her name was the *Kofuku Maru.* She had been the property of a Japanese fishing concern in Singapore and had served as fish carrier and supply ship to the sampans fishing in the area of the Anambas Islands. She was a dirty, unlovely craft, with a low freeboard, similar to many in the island fishing trade, but with her one-man Australian captain-*cum*-engineer-*cum*-navigator did wonderful service in the evacuation of Pompong.

Tall, lanky, lean-jawed, with large horn-rimmed glasses, Bill Reynolds was a character. His language was never less than lurid and to hear him castigate the crew of a trim naval launch inexpertly enough handled to bump him heavily at the Pridiraja jetty was a shrivelling experience. He had a total disrespect for all forms of authority, particularly uniformed authority, and Lyon, whose dislike of regimental forms had hardened into undisguised contempt for the orthodox warriors who had brought disaster on Singapore, took to him at once.

No two men could have been more disparate in character, but they had two further traits in common. Both loathed the Japanese and both were consumed with the idea of devising some means of returning to the area and sabotaging their occupation. The *Kofuku Maru* would be an ideal vessel to carry a guerrilla group, and Reynolds, who knew the islands intimately, an ideal man to help Lyon navigate her. Both men swore that when things got too hot they would try to get to India, join forces, and come back.

Things were indeed getting hot. One day the *Kofuku Maru* appeared no more and Lyon assumed that the indestructible Australian had decided to try out his intention of creeping north-west along the Malacca Straits to freedom. The Japanese were now in and around the islands in force. Events had overtaken Lyon's organisation far more swiftly than could have been foreseen and there was no point in hiding out on Pulau Durian just to be captured.

They held on until the last moment, and the last few days were tense. Lyon and Morris took watch and watch about during the night and had their first experience of the menace of jungle noises.

One night, just before they left, Morris, sitting on watch with his tommy gun, heard the sound of heavy bodies crashing through the bush not too far away. He quickly shook Lyon awake. "Keep me covered," said the captain, "I'll go and see what it is." He crawled forward, picked up a stone, and heaved it into the undergrowth. There were more crashing noises, but they seemed to be going away, so Lyon shone his torch, scattering a herd of wild hogs. Lyon came back laughing. "We were lucky that time anyway." Morris looked down at his gun: "Yes, weren't we, sir," he answered. Still not fully translated from medical orderly into jungle fighter, he had forgotten to put in the magazine.

When it was useless and dangerous to stay longer, Lyon and Morris boarded their dinghy one evening and themselves sailed south past the Brothers Lighthouses to the Indragiri Estuary. There was nothing for it but to roll up the pipe-line as they went. In the early hours of the morning, Lyon's sea-green eyes, which seemed to see better in the dark than those of most other men, picked out the looming shape of a destroyer off their port bow. There were no Allied destroyers left in the area, so she must be Japanese.

They sheered away to starboard, stripped down their sails, pulled out the paddle, and breathlessly cased away. Almost immediately a sister ship loomed up off the starboard bow. Fortunately a gentle tide was running in their favour, so they ducked down motionless and trusted to luck to drift past unobserved. They were not spotted by the look-outs, and once they were well clear Lyon hoisted sail again. Morris, to whom all this was entirely new, began to wonder how wise he had been to join Lyon so enthusiastically, but his qualms were soon subdued by Lyon's complete calm. The wind was now freshening, the sea rising, and they were both extremely tired. Gallantly, Morris suggested that he should take over the tiller for a while. Adaptable as he was, he felt that he could follow a compass course if Lyon set it for him.

"No thanks," said Lyon, "we would probably do much better to get a little sleep." To Morris' speechless astonishment, he unshipped the rudder, put it in the stern sheets, curled up under the thwart, and was breathing deeply on the instant. Morris took one look and decided he might as well follow suit, finding, rather to his surprise, that he dropped off immediately. When dawn broke, they awoke much refreshed in the middle of an empty sea and Lyon set course for Pridiraja.

Thence they followed their own escape route in easy stages, picking up other members at Tembilahan and Campbell at Rengat. The next stage was in icy-cold rain in an open car over the central mountain spine of Sumatra. The journey took several days, as Lyon and Campbell were calling on the Dutch officials all the way to make what arrangements they could for stay-behind parties. They found Padang still crowded with hundreds of the refugees they had passed through. The Japanese were by now crossing the island themselves, although not yet in great force, and there was no time to be lost. Somehow the Navy succeeded in rounding up a few more coastal tramps, and as soon as they were packed to the gunwales with survivors, they were despatched to the west. Morris himself was put on a small Dutch steamer of about 600 tons, with some of the survivors of the *Repulse* and *Prince of Wales*, leaving Lyon and Campbell behind.

Morris' ship had been one of the last to leave and not all its predecessors succeeded in crossing the Bay of Bengal, with Japanese bombers penetrating ever further west under strict orders to block all avenues of escape. The little ship had no means of defence, as although many of the soldiers still had their rifles, there was no ammunition for them. The ship could not make much more than eight knots, and about two days out they spotted a quantity of wreckage drifting past. There were jagged chunks of wood and, more ominously, several bloated bodies still in their life belts. The

Malay crew were afraid that it was all that was left of their sister ship, which had left ahead of them. This was confirmed the next day when a sharp-eyed lookout spotted a raft with two survivors on it. They were Javanese seamen from the sister ship and the only two men left alive out of the hundreds on board.

Morris arrived in Colombo safely and was duly ordered to return to his proper duties and report to No. 55 Combined Military Hospital. There, setting dressings and washing out bedpans again, he wondered what had happened to his companions. His liking for Lyon had developed into something approaching hero-worship. Was the captain safe? Had another ship arrived to get him away?

No further ship had put into Padang and a promised submarine had failed to arrive, but Lyon had risen to the first challenge of his astonishing career. Colonel Warren had succeeded in joining the Force 136 party, and when he saw how badly the situation was shaping, acquired a Sumatran *prahu* called the *Hin Lee*, which might enable them to make a last dash for freedom. It was a miserable craft, roughly constructed for the coastal trade, with ragged rigging and flimsy sails. About sixty feet long, it had a main hold, with a rickety "roof" made of bamboo slats, a diminutive foredeck, and a small cockpit aft for the helmsman. A sturdy, ocean-going junk can make immense voyages in complete safety, but the lightly built *Hin Lee* creaked and groaned as if she would fall apart at any moment. As much food and water as was available was put aboard and the junk moored in a nearby creek under guard.

On the evening of March 8, Warren ordered the party to sail next morning. Out of Force 136 he had selected Campbell, Lyon, Broome, Davis, and a naval lieutenant named Passmore to make the trip, as being most suitable for any guerrilla work that might later be organised from India. Place was found for eleven other officers among those still left behind in Padang. There were also two reliable Malays, who had worked with Davis and Broome. At the last moment Warren himself stayed behind to organise the resistance groups in Sumatra.

Hin Lee was leaving Padang just at the period when the north-east monsoon gives place to the south-west monsoon, a season of uncertain weather interspersed with flat calms which even the great tea clippers of the previous century had refused to sail in. Although there were five naval officers in the party, it was Lyon, the skilled yachtsman, who took over the navigation. He had with him a school atlas and, as chronometer, a clock given to him on his twenty-first birthday by his Aunt Buzz. As soon as they learnt where they were going, the native master and crew, who were still aboard, clamoured hysterically to be put ashore. In this mood they would clearly be useless and consume the valuable rations being carefully hoarded under the firm control of Jock Campbell. They were landed on a nearby island the first day out.

The ship made slow progress westwards in light airs and was twice attacked by Japanese patrol planes. Each time the Europeans crammed into the hold—it afforded no more protection than a tent—while the two Malays stayed in view, hoping to persuade the pilots that they were innocently fishing. The strategem did not work. The planes roared over them, spraying the junk with bullets, but although her hull was badly punctured, not a single man was hurt. Eighteen of them in a wooden sieve without a scratch—it seemed a miracle.

The holes were plugged and the *Hin Lee* wallowed gently westwards. With the cowardly machine-gun strafing of an unarmed junk, the iron had entered Lyon's soul. Somehow the Japanese must be made to pay for their rapacity and cruelty. He and Campbell sat together for hours, devising scores of plans for some reprisal raid. The *Hin Lee* would be useless for the purpose, but if Reynolds had succeeded in bringing out the *Kofuku Maru,* immense possibilities would be open to them. . . .

On the tenth day out they lay becalmed. Somewhere over the horizon came the thunder of a naval engagement between Allied and Japanese warships, but they sighted nothing. They had a small battery-powered wireless set with them, but it was out of order most of the time. Occasionally they picked up time signals, which confirmed the excellent time being kept by Aunt Buzz's clock and enabled them to check their position. They had made pathetically inadequate progress and, with the change in the monsoon now on them, Lyon seriously considered the possibility of returning to Sumatra with the shift in the wind and rejoining Warren.

Fortunately, light southerly airs resumed and they were able to get far enough north to pick up sufficient easterly breeze to set them in the direction of Ceylon again. By now their water supply was running perilously low and Campbell was rationing it out half a mug at a time. There was a certain amount of tinned food left, but the absence of anything fresh had lowered their appetites and caused digestive troubles. The forced inactivity in the cramped space was depriving them of the proper use of their legs and the muscles started to wither.

The wireless set had been out of action for days, and when they finally picked up another time signal, they found that they were a good hundred miles east of their calculated position. A couple of showers of rain had somewhat relieved the water shortage, but their attempts at fishing had produced only one unidentifiable creature the size of a trout. Then Brian Passmore fell overboard and was only hauled in after they had sighted the menacing triangular fin of a shark not a cable's length distant. Morale was dropping fast and if it had not been for Lyon's imperturbable courage they might have lost hope.

On April 12, after thirty-four days at sea, they sighted the mountains of Ceylon on the horizon. For two more days they edged in towards the land on a converging course, while Lyon looked for somewhere to beach the *Hin Lee*. Everyone was far too weak to swim any distance. Then, on the fourteenth, they sighted the freighter *Anglo-Canadian,* which took them aboard, fed them back to strength again, and carried them to Bombay. The *Hin Lee* was sunk by gunfire.

It had been an incredible voyage and Lyon had

emerged as the strongest personality on board. More than that, the experiences of the past two and a half months had turned him into a man with a mission. The brooding, faraway look his family and fellow officers knew so well never left him, but now he knew what he wanted.

2

THE GENESIS OF "JAYWICK"

THE HUMILIATION OF SINGAPORE SCARRED IVAN LYON FOR the rest of his short life. His hatred for the Japanese who had humbled the British Army in Malaya became a livid driving force. His green eyes would flash with anger and contempt as he piled adjective upon adjective to vilify them. He would not accept that they were invincible. What had been wrong had been the hopelessly inadequate orthodox methods of warfare employed to fight them. Now only irregular, even wildly imaginative, methods would suffice to strike back at them.

He knew the vast spaces of the South China seas, he knew the bewildering maze of islands leading up to Singapore as few men. No army and navy, not even the Japanese, could guard adequately such a vast perimeter, man the scores of thousands of miles of coastline, or control the myriad little ships which flitted like a cloud of water insects along the sea-girt archipelagoes. Given the right craft, the right crew of determined men with some resources of disguise, it must be possible to find a way through. The object could be sabotage, attacks on merchant shipping, replenishing and supplying the brave little groups of men left behind in Malaya by Force 136—anything that would harass the Japanese.

Barely recovered from the nightmare of the *Hin Lee*, Lyon and Campbell reported to Domba House in New Delhi, the scratch headquarters of the resuscitated Force 136, which, when the tide of war finally started to turn, became one of the largest agent-dropping and sabotage organisations in the Allied armies. But that was not yet. In the spring of 1942, they were at their wits' end how to operate at all. It was not only Malaya that had been lost, but the Japanese were overrunning Burma. The puny wireless sets left with the stay-behind parties would only reach as far as Rangoon, and Rangoon in its turn had fallen. There was no way of coordinating their activities and no way of reaching them.

There were no planes available with sufficient range. The Malacca Straits on the west coast of Malaya were so shallow as to be unsuitable for submarine operations and all the approaches had been heavily mined by the Japanese. The two Dutch submarines that remained to the Allied navies were fully engaged in trying to halt the Japanese warships now roaming freely in the Indian Ocean.

Only Lyon had an answer. Singapore must be reached through the *back door,* up through the Lombok Straits, east of Java, from Australia. He had the ship with which to do it. The incredible Reynolds, with a scratch Chinese crew, had crept up the coast of Sumatra in the *Kofuku Maru* through those same Malacca

Straits and had brought her to India. This battered, gawky, decrepit craft, sister to scores of others throughout the South Seas, could take them back again.

At first the idea was dismissed as a pipe dream. What damage could she do? She could carry neither enough stores nor enough men to do anything worth while. Who would sail in her and who would command her? Lyon?—a soldier? Nonsense!

The chair-borne planners and staff officers reckoned without Lyon's quiet persistence. Opposition and obstruction only served to strengthen his single-mindedness. The scheme he and Campbell had concocted was in all conscience crazy enough. They proposed to penetrate the outer defences of Singapore in the *Kofuku Maru*, launch trained commandos in collapsible canoes to paddle into the Roads by night, attach limpet mines to the shipping in the harbour, and make their getaway by the same route. Doggedly they hawked the plan around. Lyon never took no for an answer. If one staff officer proved intractable, he went to another branch on another tack. Still a very junior officer, he impudently button-holed very senior ones with his obsession. He even succeeded in seeing the then General Sir Archibald Wavell, Commander-in-Chief India, whose one eye had always gleamed benevolently on unorthodox warriors.

In a sub-continent desperately on the defensive, here at least was one positive idea for taking the offensive. Admiral Sir Geoffrey Layton, C.-in-C. Ceylon, and Admiral Sir Geoffrey Arbuthnot, C.-in-C. East Indies Station, both gave their backing and things started to move. But the planning and organisation must be done in Australia, where the problems of security could be more easily mastered than in a loyalty-torn India.

Remembering the faithful Taffy Morris, Lyon went down to Ceylon to recruit his services for the second time, but the commanding officer of No. 55 Combined Military Hospital would not hear of it. Lyon was not to be deterred. A combination of subtle pressure organised from New Delhi soon had the delighted Morris liberated. He was quickly transferred on paper to the Indian Army Corps of Clerks, to enable him to carry arms legally. That made two officers and one man, which was a beginning. There was also Bill Reynolds, presiding blasphemously over the reconditioning of the *Kofuku Maru* at Bombay. For rather obvious reasons, she had been renamed *Krait*. As soon as she was more seaworthy, Reynolds made two attempts to sail her to Australia. Twice the engine broke down, and in the end she was loaded on the deck of an itinerant tramp for Sydney. Campbell and Morris went ahead in the *Athlone Castle*, which was carrying part of the Australian 9th Division back from the Middle East.

Lyon also had gone ahead, to report to the Services Reconnaissance Department in Melbourne, the Australian section of the organisation slowly spreading its network of saboteurs and resistance workers throughout the enemy-held world, the Special Operations Executive.

The news that greeted his arrival provided the ultimate link in his savage hatred of the Japanese. A few days earlier, Gabrielle Lyon, with her infant son, tired of waiting disconsolately at Perth for the husband she knew to be in India, had sailed in the liner *Nankin* to join him. On the way, her ship, with a cargo of explosives, had been spotted by a Japanese aircraft and intercepted by a German raider. A straddled salvo had enforced surrender and all the passengers and crew had been captured. Well treated by the Germans, whose doctor took special care of little Clive's teething troubles, they were soon transferred to the ungentle hands of the Japanese, who interned Mrs. Lyon in Tokyo for the rest of the war.

Lyon never saw his wife and son again. It was nearly a year, when the German raider herself was captured, before the fate of her prisoners was known. Interviewed over the Australian radio in Melbourne about the tragedy, Ivan Lyon commented in one short clipped sentence: "War is a grim business, isn't it?"

Now nothing could deter him from his fixed purpose, not even the renewed obstructionism of a new headquarters. General Douglas MacArthur's South West Pacific Area Command had only been set up in April 1942, after the fall of the Philippines. Grimly engaged in holding the line of New Guinea and the Solomon Islands in order to protect the precious supply route from America to Australia, there was little time to pay serious attention to a proposed sabotage raid thousands of miles to the west. Their only requirement was to reinforce the priceless chain of "coast watchers," trained, isolated jungle fighters farsightedly planted up the eastern island chain by the Australian Army before the Pacific Front collapsed. With their faithful natives and their hand-cranked wireless sets, they were able to give such accurate information of Japanese air and naval movements that the depleted Allied forces were always able to concentrate at the crucial point during those desperate days.

India Command may have approved the venture and might be sending down the precious folboats and supplies, but the line of demarcation between Wavell and MacArthur ran through Malaya, which lay at the extreme limit of the two perimeters they were trying to hold. Communication between them was infrequent and what was sponsored by the one did not necessarily attract any notice in the other.

Lyon and Jock Campbell endured several cruelly frustrating weeks. Staff officers would fob them off, their requests for supplies would be put at the bottom of the pile, the equipment they needed was always earmarked for use elsewhere. Taut, nervy, and unsmiling, his cheeks hollow from the constant strain, Lyon haunted Allied headquarters, where most of the officers thought him an eccentric nuisance.

The Services Reconnaissance Department, still an embryo organisation and with little influence, was housed in a forbidding grey mansion behind a high wall, called Airlie, in the wealthy Melbourne suburb of Toorak. The C.O., Lieutenant-Colonel G. S. Mott, was guardedly sympathetic to Lyon and Campbell, but it needed a convincing demonstration to jerk General Headquarters out of their disinterest. To accomplish this the S.R.D. played a risky trick. An Australian commando captain named Carey, from the secret training station far up the Queensland coast at Townsville, was told to carry out a mock limpet attack in the Roads, now growing as a trans-shipment centre for supplies and full of merchant shipping.

With a few companions he rowed round the harbour at night, planting his dummy limpets everywhere. Memories of the recent Japanese midget-submarine attack in Sydney Harbour were sufficiently alive for one ship, more alert than the others, to sound the alarm. The ensuing panic was homeric. Action stations were sounded, sirens wailed, searchlights flashed, and the town was blacked out until the hoax was discovered. Certain port security officers found themselves transferred and the attitude of G.H.Q. was transformed.

Lyon, in the meantime, had lost no opportunity of lobbying the great. His elder sister, Ann Gordon, married to an Australian naval officer, had travelled out with Mrs. Casey, the mother of the future External Affairs Minister. Ivan Lyon had asked his sister if she could recommend him to any influential people in Australia, and Mrs. Casey had been the first name she gave him. He did not really need the introduction. Mrs. Casey was sitting in the lounge of the Menzies Hotel one day and was so struck with the appearance and bearing of a young Highland officer who walked in that she asked someone his name. Realising who he was, she invited him over and enquired if there was any way in which she could help him. He asked if she could possibly introduce him to Lord Gowrie, V.C., the greatly beloved Governor-General. "But he's coming to dinner with us tomorrow evening," said Mrs. Casey, "you must come and join us."

Lyon was still only a major, but his curious combination of intensity and charm worked again. Appreciating his true qualities, Lord Gowrie took him under his wing and soon the difficulties started to melt away. The hare-brained scheme was officially baptised Operation "Jaywick," although no one seems to remember how the name arose.

Soon Campbell and Lyon were installed in a flat in Sydney, with Morris, resplendent in Australian Army uniform, with a Great Britain flash, as their general factotum. It was now well into autumn, and it was Lyon's dream to carry out his attack on Singapore on February 15, 1943, the anniversary of the surrender. The men would be recruited from naval ratings and soldiers who had volunteered for unspecified "hazardous service" and were taking commando courses at the Army Physical and Recreational Training School at Frankston, Victoria. Bill Reynolds would be the navigator and they would need at least two more officers to train as operatives with Lyon for the two-man canoes they would be taking with them.

They had glowing recommendations about an R.N.V.R. lieutenant who had also sailed his way out of Singapore, named Donald Davidson, and went down to Sydney to meet him. Off the train came a tall, spare officer in naval uniform with a long, rather haggard face, wearing a monocle. As they crossed the street outside, he tripped over the kerb and measured his length on the asphalt, with his eyeglass tinkling down the gutter ahead of him. First impressions were deceptive. Fantastically tough, utterly fearless, a born organiser, he was a very lucky find indeed. Second in command on both Lyon's expeditions, he was a perfect foil, with his boundless energy, drive, and enthusiasm, to the less robust, more introspective Gordon Highlander.

Lyon did the basic thinking and planning, and Davidson put it into effect. Educated at Cheltenham, he had been a sheep-and-cattle farmer in western Queensland and a teak merchant in Burma. Now thirty-five, he had spent most of his life out of doors, knew the jungle and the ways of natives, was an expert sailor, and could read a chart upside down at dead of night and never lose his way.

They set up a tented training camp in Refuge Bay, an inlet in Broken Bay, the estuary of the Hawkesbury River, north of Sydney. It was in a small gully through which flowed a crystal-clear stream, plunging a hundred feet over the cliff into the cove below—miles from anywhere and completely isolated. Their only communication with the outside world was a little outboard dinghy, which would take them three or four miles across the estuary to the small jetty which was their roadhead from Sydney.

It was bush country and they first had to clear the site. Morris, the ex-miner, rather fancied himself with an axe or a *parang*, but when he found Davidson could keep up with him stroke for stroke, he lost all reservations about that monocle. It was only an amiable affectation.

On September 19, 1942, Lyon thought he had better prepare his parents for what might lie ahead. He warned them that in the future there would be periods of many months when they did not hear from him. All he could tell them was that recent events had made him very angry and that he would not be wasting his time.

There were about twenty of them in the party to start with, although this was winnowed down and further changes made before the expedition was finally launched. The three seamen operatives, each a bow man to the officer in each folboat, were there from the beginning. Falls, the oldest of them, and therefore called "Poppa," although he was only twenty-three, was a magnificent specimen, with the build and looks of a young Greek god. Even-tempered, with an old head on his shoulders, he had been a dairy farmer and was a steadying influence on the younger ones. There was a tremendous solid strength about him, with an underlying hint of hidden violence, a man you would want to be on your side in a fight. He would take all the ragging and horseplay good-naturedly, but no one ever made the mistake of carrying things too far.

"Arty" Jones was another find. Short, thickset, and dark, he could be taken from a distance for a Japanese —something that might prove useful. Yet he was pure Australian from Perth and had been a grocer's assistant. He could turn his hand to anything and did everything well. He could drink his beer and swap rough jokes with the rest of them, but he was fundamentally serious, without the ready sense of humour of the rest.

Huston, the baby of the party—he was seventeen—was, to begin with, an unknown quantity. They called him "Happy" because he did not laugh very much, but he took tremendous pains and became such a reliable member of the party that Lyon chose him as his own partner. He had to do everything from scratch, even learning to swim. His final choice for the expedition was due to the fact that he was always looking for something useful to do, a valuable characteristic for a little party that might soon have more on its hands than it could manage.

The rest were to form part of the actual crew of *Krait*. "Cobber" Cain, the bosun's mate, was a huge fellow, built like a long-distance swimmer except that the generous chest and stomach that looked like fat were solid muscle. An easy-going rolling stone, he had been a market gardener, a bartender, but had become a superb seaman, who could splice a rope, caulk a seam, improvise, and run a taut ship. With Falls, he was the steadiest man aboard, although, like the others, he was always a little jealous of the glamour surrounding the actual operatives.

"Biffo" Marsh was the practical joker of the party. Strong as an ox, he was always slapping people on the back, tripping them up, wrestling them down, hiding snakes in their beds, and generally playing hell. His good humour was so contagious that he was the most popular man in the party. He never minded being thumped back and one irreverent member always does a small group of people good. He had been, of all things, a cabinet maker's apprentice, and the last member of the first group of trainees, "Moss" Berryman, had been a shop assistant in Adelaide. Quiet, dependable, and utterly reliable, he was, with Marsh, one of the reserve operatives and was bitterly disappointed that he did not take part in the actual attack.

Such, then, was the human material Lyon had to weld into a sabotage force to strike deep into the heartland of the Japanese-held empire: teak farmer, shop assistants, a bartender, and a few tough young men from the Australian outback. Everything had to be improvised, tactics, training, equipment, camouflage, routes, and methods. They would be in enemy-controlled waters for anything up to six weeks and would have to cover at least four thousand miles from their Australian launching point. They were going into an area where every white man was automatically recognisable as an enemy. Apart from painting their bodies, *Krait* would be almost their only disguise, and she would have to sail under the Japanese flag to avoid immediate challenge.

The canoe crews, once launched as near to Singapore as possible, would have to travel and attack by night and hide by day, involving back-breaking porterages. They would have to carry all their own food and water as well as heavy loads of ammunition and mines. The crews would have to talk in whispers, never show a light, and navigate by dead reckoning among the bewildering currents and tide-rips of the Indonesian archipelago. Viewed sanely, the task appeared impossible, yet Lyon solved it, trying all the tactics out himself first with Davidson, testing and continually modifying the equipment and hardening up his taut body to match the physical feats of his men.

The training was ferocious. The object was to bring everyone to the pinnacle of human fitness and endurance. Most of the time they went round in bare feet, until they grew so hardened that they could scale the cliffs, track each other through the bush, and clamber over the barnacle-covered rocks in the cove without a single laceration. In return they fed like fighting cocks, and when Morris used to take the dinghy over to the roadhead to fetch the supplies, the rest of them would clamber up the cliff face with a sack of flour on their backs rather than take the easy way round by a path.

Morris himself nearly came to grief that way. He was hauling himself over an overhanging ledge when he came face to face with an iguana, which had been basking in the sun. These big lizards can inflict a nasty bite, but just as Morris recovered sufficiently from the shock to save himself from a seventy-foot drop, the iguana took equal fright at this sudden apparition and scuttled off.

They practised unarmed combat, sometimes with visiting instructors from Sydney, until the men could run full tilt at each other with bare knives, broken bottles, revolvers, and bayonets and never reach their mark. They learned to make straight for a sentry's eyes, joints, and private parts. Campbell by this time had become the administrative officer of the expedition in Sydney and spent little time at the camp, but Lyon and Davidson trained with the others and became as nimble as the rest.

They were dumped fifty miles away in the bush without a compass at night and taught to find their way home by the stars and such natural marks as the side of a tree on which moss will grow. They learned to stalk each other and freeze immobile for minutes on end, to move soundlessly and melt into a dark background. Half a dozen of them would take out a storm lantern into the surrounding bush which the rest were required to reach, snuff out, and carry back. In all this Davidson was the task master. He was insatiable and unwearying, lashing them until their last ounce of strength had gone, but asking no one to do what he would not do himself. He roughed it and tussled with the men, fought them with his bare hands in unarmed combat, raced with them, climbed trees with them, and was their match in everything. He was always doing something, making rough clothing, sewing, repairing, whittling, sorting the stores, a human dynamo. The monocle was seldom clamped in his eye now.

The main recreation was swimming in the shark-infested bay. One of them used to sit on top of the cliff with a whistle, a telescope, and a Bren gun. If he saw a shark approaching he would blow the whistle, fire off a magazine around it, and scare it off. By the time the folboats arrived, they were almost hardened enough to swim to Singapore.

Now came the next phase in the training. These

remarkable collapsible boats, rubberised canvas on a bamboo frame, with brass screw mountings on the end of each member, were built like kayaks, with two round holes in the top into which the paddlers were laced. About seventeen feet long and less than a yard wide when assembled, they could carry up to an astonishing 800 pounds' weight of man and stores. Broken down they weighed about 70 pounds, an easy load for two men to lift and not too much for a fit man to carry. They found it easiest with a head-band, native fashion. Their maintenance needed careful attention. Rough sand or rock would soon scrape the canvas, although it could be mended like a punctured inner tube. They had to be washed out inside after each launching or sand lodged between the bamboo frame and the skin would soon rub the canvas dangerously thin.

Paddles were another problem. In tropical waters each stroke can leave a phosphorescent swirl. They found that brackish water near the shore was the least affected. In the beam of a searchlight, the flash of a paddle-blade in the air can be seen a couple of miles or more away. In the end they settled for the Canadian type of single paddle, with a knob on the handle and a three-foot blade. This never leaves the water except when aching arms demand a change of side, and if whittled razor-sharp at the edge, glides through the back stroke like an eel.

Once they mastered the folboats, they rode the water like sea gulls. The "Jaywick" party practised with them endlessly, beaching them, jumping in and out of them in the water, capsizing them and righting them again, breaking them down, assembling them at night, carrying them long distances, and camouflaging them in the bush. They became so proficient that they could paddle them ten hours a day and sometimes used to take them right out of Broken Bay into the Pacific rollers, riding the surf and then relaunching them. Once they had learnt the trick of not breaking the canoe's back on a roller they could slide them up and down the troughs and waves like corks.

The final stage was to practise with their offensive weapon, the limpet mine. This is an ingenious object about the size of a dinner plate, in which hangs suspended a container of high explosive shaped like a quart milk bottle. Round the edge are four powerful magnets on hinged springs. They were used in groups of three, joined by seventy-five feet of cordtex fuse, and carried in waterproof containers between and on either side of the aft paddler's legs—a tight fit.

The method of attack was to drift down the side of a ship with the tide or current, the rear canoeist securing the canoe with a magnetised hold-fast, while his companion slid the mines down a placing stick five feet under water. The magnets would make an audible clang as they snapped home, but then it needed a crowbar to release them. They could be fired singly by a time fuse consisting of a phial of acid dripping on copper wire, or sympathetically in groups of two or three if connected with the lengths of cordtex. The whole operation took about twenty minutes.

On a merchant ship, each would blow a hole about five feet in diameter, and if correctly placed against the holds, three must inevitably sink her. The only type of ship against which they were relatively ineffective were tankers, where the tamping effect of the liquid cargo would only result in a hole about a foot in diameter. Unless the oil caught fire, which, curiously enough, was seldom, it would slowly mix with the sea water and the tanker would retain its buoyancy. Even so, it could be crippled with mines placed against the propeller shaft and engine room. The operatives wore skin-tight black vests and hoods and with their slate-grey folboats and paddles were almost invisible at night, except in the direct beam of a searchlight, which would pick them up, even bow on, up to 1800 yards away.

The folboats also enabled them to indulge in a modest social life. They would paddle about ten miles across Refuge Bay to two little resorts called Little and Big Potonga, which attracted week-enders from Sydney and even provided a village concert hall with a piano. The beer was good, but the ten-mile paddle back kept them sober, although one night Biffo Marsh felt sufficiently inspired to put a dead snake in Poppa Falls' bed. To everyone's surprise Falls tucked himself in comfortably and went straight off to sleep. Then, at five o'clock in the morning, they were all awakened by a blood-curdling yell. There was Falls thundering round the camp, threatening to strangle the man who had played such a trick on him. His language made even the hardened Australians shudder, and when they finally quietened him down, thought it better not to name the perpetrator. He never did find out.

They had also acquired a mascot. One day, quite early on, to their astonishment a beautiful white Persian cat wandered out of the bush. She was dubbed Cleopatra. The attraction was mutual and she became a general favourite, although they had to keep her claws away from the folboats. They could not imagine where she had come from, as there was no human habitation within ten miles. They were even more amazed when she deposited four kittens on Morris' pyjamas, as there was no tom cat within a day's march, much less a Persian one. As soon as the kittens were big enough they were in their turn distributed as mascots to the naval corvettes which used to come and anchor on the other side of Refuge Bay.

These corvettes also provided willing targets for Lyon's dummy attacks by folboat at night. By now the "Jaywick" crews were so well trained and confident that Lyon gleefully accepted a challenge from the captain of one of the corvettes that they would not succeed in attacking his ship on a given night without detection. It was agreed that the corvette's crew should be on the alert at any time at night from ten o'clock onwards. The next morning Lyon paddled over and greeted the captain, who leant over the side and said: "I think you owe me a bottle of whisky."

"With pleasure," Lyon called over, "but may I collect my painters first." To the captain's chagrin he paddled round collecting one from the rudder, one from the propeller shaft, one from the anchor chain, until he had half a dozen in his fist. The naval captain ruefully gave him best and the bottle of whisky went the other way.

They were just as silent and effective on land. There was a gun battery on the promontory facing Lion Island out in Broken Bay. Here it was Campbell who issued a friendly challenge to the officer in charge. There were two hundred men in the battery, and the twenty men of "Jaywick" offered to take over the whole position. Neither side was to take any action until a Very light was fired at ten o'clock at night. It was too easy. Morris and another commando landed in a folboat about two miles away from the machine-gun posts which guarded one extremity of their camp. These were about fifty yards apart on the side of a hill. The two of them crawled up gullies undetected to the rear of these posts. Morris even heard the commander of the guard exhorting the gunner to keep his eyes skinned, as the commandos must be due to strike soon.

As soon as the officer had gone, Morris slid down from behind a bush and stuck his revolver in the man's back. He duly surrendered. Then, on the field telephone, Morris called up the next post. Assuming an Australian accent, he asked the next man to come over and lend a hand, as he could hear someone rustling in the trees behind him. The second gunner was duly neutralised and in no time he had the six of them in the bag. The rest of the party had intercepted the ration wagon which came during the night from Sydney, locked up the driver and his mate, dressed two of the commandos in their clothes, drove through the gates, and took over the guardhouse and the telephone exchange. Relaying a series of false orders, they soon had all two hundred men rounded up without firing a shot. That exploit was reported to General Headquarters. It was obviously high time for the "Jaywick" party to leave.

They were getting a little too high-spirited for local comfort. One afternoon a civilian yacht chose to sail into their particular corner of Refuge Bay. It had no business to come round the point, but the warning suggested by Davidson was a little drastic. He quickly had one of the Bren guns mounted, which fired a sharp burst of tracer bullets across the yacht's bows.

The Governor-General himself came round to pay them a farewell visit before they left, accompanied by General Sir Thomas Blamey, the Commander-in-Chief Land Forces, South West Pacific Area. It was a mortifying day for Morris, who, in addition to being medical orderly, was quartermaster, general handyman, and O.C. dinghy. When the distinguished visitors came to leave, duly impressed by the superb quality of the men they had inspected, Morris cheerfully carried out Lord Gowrie, whose V.C. impressed him more than his weight, on his shoulders to the dinghy, but as soon as everyone was settled in, the engine spluttered to a standstill. It was the first time this had ever happened. Furiously, Morris tugged, time and time again, at the starting thong on the fly wheel. He could not raise a single cough. Just as he was getting too hot, bothered, and embarrassed to contain himself,

Lord Gowrie leant over and said: "Patience, my boy, patience. We quite appreciate how you feel, if it would help relieve you, say it." This was the Gowrie touch. It had charmed eight million Australians and worked just as well with a Welsh coal miner. Grinning sheepishly, Morris gave it up, sat in the stern sheets, and paddled his valuable cargo to the launch. Once they were aboard he gave the starting handle a final vicious tug. Naturally the engine sprang into steady thrumming life. He could cheerfully have dropped it into the cove in his fury, when Lord Gowrie leant over the rail of the launch and asked: "Taffy, what part of Scotland do you come from?" It was the sort of thing that had made the Australians keep him as their governor for eight mutually appreciative years.

On January 16, 1943, *Krait* came chugging into Refuge Bay, with Bill Reynolds, haggard, humourous, and blasphemous as ever, at the wheel. She had been undergoing a major refit in the Sydney dockyards and now was ready for their long journey. Cheers rent the cove, salvos from the Bren and Owen submachine guns echoed round the bay, and everybody tumbled down the rocks, launched every boat, and boarded her.

At this stage, none of the party, with the exception of Lyon, Davidson, Campbell, and Reynolds, knew where they were going. For security reasons, they had been given to understand that the tactics they had been learning were for an attack in the Roads of Surabaya, at the eastern end of Java, not too far inside the Lombok Straits. The word "Singapore" had never been mentioned. Wherever they were going,

Krait was a welcome sight. They had reached the limit of their training and welcomed a change of scene.

The folboats, limpets, and essential stores were quickly loaded into the forward hold. Hammocks, mattresses, and blankets were already aboard and no man took more than a small kit bag of personal effects. The Refuge Bay camp was left to be struck by other hands. At dawn the following day the expedition headed out of Broken Bay and turned north on the first leg of their voyage round Australia to their launching base on the north-west corner of the continent at Exmouth Gulf.

Krait may have had an engine overhaul, but apart from a few structural alterations on deck under the awning, she remained the same dirty little fishing craft Lyon and Reynolds had used in the evacuation of the Singapore refugees a year earlier. The hull was painted a rusty black. Her foremast carried an auxiliary sail rolled up on its boom. Amidships was the enclosed wheelhouse, leaving only about eighteen inches of her eleven-foot beam on either side. The awning which covered the whole of the afterdeck was made of wood overlaid with tar paper. Under it was the engine house, about eight feet square, and in the stern a primitive "head" on the port side and the enclosed galley on the starboard side, with a few shelves for pots and pans and a couple of oil burners. Narrow-gutted for her seventy-foot length, she was a bad sea boat, but she was solidly built of teak and the extra fuel tanks which had been crammed in gave her a range of 8000 miles. Her maximum speed was seven knots.

The deck was littered with forty-four-gallon drums of kerosene and unstowed cargo. The fore hold was full of their operational stores, food for twenty men for six months and immense quantities of ammunition. The second small hold amidships had been converted to house three bunks and the aircraft-type wireless receiver and transmitter. It was officers' mess, chart room, sick bay, signals office, and store room in one. In the wheelhouse a substantial seat had been built athwartships, behind the helmsman, to accommodate the off-watch navigator. The rest of the living space consisted of half a dozen hammocks slung from the awning and four mattresses on top of the engine-room housing. Organised into two watches under Lyon and Davidson, there was just room for the crew to move around without getting hopelessly in each other's way.

They had engine trouble with the elderly German Deutz diesel from the start. The second day, after wallowing crazily in the swell, they were towed ingloriously into Newcastle with a seized-up clutch. No sooner was that repaired than the bilge pumps started to foul. When this was rectified they had to put in to Coffs Harbour with choked lubricating pipes, which caused the fore bearing to seize. No spares were to be had for the old engine, but it was patched up enough to get them to Brisbane by the end of the month. By now another major overhaul was necessary and Lyon's dream of an attack on Singapore on February 15 became impossible. It was a bitter blow, but in no way altered his determination to get there as soon as they could. Campbell came up to join them from Sydney, and while the repairs were being done to *Krait,* most of the crew spent their time at Surfer's Paradise, the handsome Pacific bathing beach near Brisbane, toughening themselves up in the breakers and acquiring a deep tan which might stand them in useful stead once they were in enemy waters.

At the beginning of March they were off again, but their troubles were not yet ended. Running into a violent storm off Moreton Island, they learned the true vagaries of *Krait*'s behaviour in heavy weather. She was the worst sea boat imaginable. With her narrow beam and eighteen inches of freeboard, she behaved like a drunken, sluggish submarine. It was as much as they could do to hold her head to the seas, and as she groaned and rolled, everything not firmly lashed down was washed overboard. Their losses included the unfortunate Cleo. One moment she was huddled against the bulwarks on the foredeck and after the next heavy sea came inboard she was gone. It was almost worse than losing onc of the crew.

They never reached Townsville, their next stage, under their own power. A day's sail away, the worn-out Deutz diesel gave one shattering final bang and stopped dead. One of the pistons had forced its way through the engine casing. Again they had to suffer the ignominy of a tow, not only to Townsville, where the useless engine was removed, but empty further north to Cairns. Here they spent another two months, while a replacement engine was sought and the crew were sent to the nearby commando training school to keep themselves fit.

One piece of news compensated Lyon for all these setbacks. It was confirmed with certainty that Gaby and the boy were relatively safe in civilian internment in Japan. Ivan had high hopes of getting her exchanged, but he was even more determined to repay the Japanese for what she had suffered. He also learned that he had received the M.B.E. for his work in Sumatra. Although he had the assurance of the Director of Naval Intelligence that everything possible had been done to get Gaby a place in the next exchange ship, this never happened, but the thought of it buoyed up Lyon amidst his frustration. He had planned to sail to Singapore and sail to Singapore he would.

Australia was combed for a new engine and a suitable one was finally discovered in Tasmania, a brand-new 105-h.p. Gardner diesel. He also made the final changes in the personnel of the expedition. Rather unfairly perhaps, he blamed Bill Reynolds for much of their engine trouble, although it was probably just as well that they made no attempt to carry out the plan with such an elderly hunk of metal. Reynolds, so much older than the rest of them, had not fitted in too well either with officers or men. It was a hard decision, but the man who had brought *Krait* from Singapore to India and from Sydney nearly to the northern tip of Australia, was replaced.

His successor proved a gem, a stringy old Ulster Scot from Belfast named "Paddy" McDowell. He had served in Q-ships in the First World War, and his subsequent wanderings had brought him to Australia and his present exalted rank in the Navy of Leading Stoker. He was a wonderful engineer, who nursed the new diesel like a baby, running his sensitive fingers over it in the dark to forestall the slightest shiver or sign of overheating. The hideously hot little engine room became his home and he only emerged with reluctance to let Biffo Marsh take over from time to time. With his salty ways and outrageous old sailor's anecdotes, he became one of the major characters aboard.

They also acquired a new telegraphist, a slight, pale, dedicated boy named Young. He was as devoted to his wireless set as Paddy McDowell was to his engine and would sit tirelessly for hours maintaining watch at his knobs, cooped up in the tiny cabin amidships with barely headroom. If a sea was running and the hatch was open, most of the water fell on Young, but he never complained. Calm and completely reliable, he studied a correspondence course in wireless telegraphy throughout the cruise, even in enemy waters, and on his return passed his examination.

The "Jaywick" party had also been strengthened by two new officers. "Ted" Carse came as navigator and ship's captain. A quiet, rather morose individual, with a lined, sad face, he had served with the Royal Australian Navy for some years between the two wars but had then retired, taking up odd jobs in Australia and the South Sea Islands. He had prospected for gold, fished for *bêche-de-mer*, and had then started his own, quite prosperous, imitation-jewellery firm.

Called back from the reserve, he was chosen for the expedition because of his intimate knowledge of taking small craft round the archipelagoes of the South Seas. He was not in the best of health and his eyesight was starting to give him trouble, yet he had an underlying dogged persistence and professional pride which enabled him, almost more than any other man, to get the operatives to their destination and back.

The best piece of luck was finding Lieutenant Page of the A.I.F. He came from a well-known and much respected Australian family. His uncle was Sir Earle Page, and his father, Major Harold Page, had been assistant administrator of Australian New Guinea. Captured by the Japanese, he had lost his life when the transport *Montevideo Maru* was torpedoed by an Allied submarine while carrying prisoners to Japan.

"Bob" Page had been at Sydney University and was in his third year as a medical student when he joined the forces. Quiet and serious most of the time, he had an engaging sense of humour and real powers of leadership. Somehow his presence welded together the British and Australian members of the expedition. Trained in commando tactics and a successful "coast watcher," he became the third officer operative with Lyon and Davidson and formed an ideal team with Arty Jones. Page also shared with Lyon and Davidson the motive of personal revenge against the Japanese. One had lost a father, the other's wife and child were prisoners, and Davidson's two brothers had been captured by the Japanese in Malaya.

The last member of the expedition to join was almost an afterthought. Lyon had made up his mind that the party needed a cook. It looked like being a thankless task and he only obtained one volunteer from the local commando school. This was a Sapper corporal named Andy or "Jock" Crilly, who was more attracted by the promise of adventure than by the opportunity of practising the culinary arts. He was given three days to learn his trade, and the only thing he was sure of was his pancakes, which he had cooked as a boy in the outback at his home near Toowoomba.

Most of his duties consisted in opening tins, which was not too difficult, and brewing up navy *kai*, which he soon learnt from Paddy McDowell. The menu usually consisted of dehydrated vegetables, onions, and meat, which had to be soaked for hours before providing an unpalatable mess. Not even an Escoffier could have improved upon such raw materials. In the long months ahead, Crilly never let his companions down. Cramped in his ridiculous galley, with his pots and pans sliding from side to side of the primitive stove, slopping over, scalding him, and generally making his life a hell, he never failed to come up with three hot meals a day, whatever the weather, whatever the danger, and whatever the state of his often outraged Scottish temper.

Morris was delighted to have him aboard, and they formed an inseparable army minority of two. In the clannish way of servicemen, Marsh, Berryman, and

Huston formed another little group, and Jones and Falls made up another pair.

It was August 1943 before *Krait* was finally ready for sea and the official roll of her complement read thus:

Maj. I. Lyon, Gordon Highlanders	C.O.
Lt. D. N. Davidson, R.N.V.R.	1st Lt.
Lt. H. C. Carse, R.A.N.V.R.	Navigator
Lt. R. C. Page, A.I.F.	M.O.
A/Ldg. Seaman K. P. Cain, R.A.N.	Ships Staff
Ldg. Stoker J. P. McDowell, R.N.	1st Engineer
Ldg. Telegraphist H. S. Young, R.A.N.	Wireless Operator
Cpl. R. G. Morris, R.A.M.C.	Medical Orderly
Cpl. A. Crilly, A.I.F.	Cook
A/Able Seaman W. C. Falls, R.A.N.	Operative
A/Able Seaman A. W. Jones, R.A.N.	Operative
A/Able Seaman A. W. G. Huston, R.A.N.	Operative
A/Able Seaman F. W. Marsh, R.A.N.	2nd Engineer
A/Able Seaman M. Berryman, R.A.N.	Deck Hand

They still seemed a motley crew for such a fantastic enterprise, but Lyon had picked his men well. From beginning to end their magnificent morale never faltered and they left in high spirits, duly fortified by the party they held to celebrate the birth of Young's daughter. He had been more than a little worried about his wife's health, but now that all was well, he became one of the steadiest members of the party.

The greatest disappointment was their slow speed. The new engine seemed to have made no difference and they could never coax more than seven knots out of it. The trouble seemed to be with the propeller, which appeared only to slice the water above a certain number of revolutions. Time was pressing now and there was no hope of further replacements. Even hoisting the sail made little difference and merely increased their silhouette. It took the best part of three weeks for the grossly overloaded ship to reach Exmouth Gulf. As they rounded Thursday Island at the northern tip of the York Peninsula, they suffered their first casualty. Morris was keeping watch, standing on the fuel tank under the after awning, with his head and shoulders out of the hatchway, when there was an explosion. As the medical orderly, he immediately ducked down to see what had happened. "Anybody hurt?" he enquired, and then found, rather to his surprise, that he had suffered the worst damage himself.

Cobber Cain had been cleaning one of their Owen submachine guns when a round became jammed in the breech and exploded. It shattered a bottle, peppering Morris and Berryman with thousands of tiny splinters. A jagged piece of metal had hit Morris in the ankle. He had felt nothing until the nasty wound was pointed out to him. Blood was spurting out, so the rest of them grabbed him, carried him to the fore hatch, where Page swiftly applied a tourniquet and got out the needle and catgut. They had no anaesthetics and gave Morris a bottle of brandy instead. By now he was semi-conscious with secondary shock, and although there was quite a high sea running and the surgeon and his assistants were drenched by the incoming waves, Page performed a neat job. He dusted the wound with sulfanilamide powder and had Morris carried down to a bunk in his own sick bay. With the deck continually awash, Morris' ankle never entirely healed, but he refused all suggestions that he be put ashore and limped uncomplainingly through the entire expedition.

Krait's freeboard was now lower than ever, as Lyon, with unpleasant memories of the *Hin Lee*, had been persuaded to instal a layer of plastic concrete four inches thick over the whole foredeck as anti-aircraft protection. The extra weight made her so unmanageable that they chipped it off and threw it overboard. Their firepower was probably sufficient defence anyway. They had two Lewis guns, two Bren guns, a dozen Owen submachine guns, and could give good account of themselves. At action stations in home waters these were distributed at strategic points round the deck or poked through the hatches in the after awning. As soon as they got into enemy waters, everyone except Carse at the wheel, Davidson beside him, Young at his wireless set, and Paddy McDowell in the engine room, would be concentrated under the awning, ready to fire through gun ports in the bulwarks when danger threatened.

They had also practised a final desperate measure should they be challenged by a patrol craft. The dinghy had been fitted with an air tube through the keel, and the plan was for Jones, who could pass for a Japanese, and Lyon, who might be taken for a Malay once he was stained with the camouflage paint they were carrying, to paddle round to the far side of the enemy with two of the other operatives clinging to the keel, armed with limpet mines. These would be planted with a short fuse and the rest of the crew would open up with every available gun in the hope of sinking their adversary with all hands.

Apart from celebrating Lyon's twenty-eighth birthday on August 17, they had settled down to a comfortable shipboard routine. There was normally someone off watch sleeping under the awning, so those who wanted to yarn, or play cards on a calm day, would go up on the foredeck. Most of them had run out of original conversation long since, but if the hatch cover above Young's head was open, they could usually persuade him to tune in to some radio station and give them a concert of music or the latest news. What reading material they had brought with them had been read and reread and the radio was almost their only amusement. They were already starting to accustom themselves to native clothing. Their own uniforms had been left behind at Townsville with Campbell, who had returned to Melbourne to act as rear link, and they either wore nondescript shorts and shirts or rolled a *sarong* round their waist. Shoes they had discarded as unnecessary. The deck of *Krait* was as smooth as a cricket pitch compared with the barnacles of Refuge Bay.

Japanese aircraft were known to be operating in the area of Cape Wessel, but *Krait* was not attacked and the rest of the first lap was uneventful. With Davidson and Carse meticulously plotting the uncharted reefs along the unfrequented coast—they crossed one of them in dead of night round Adele Island, where there was supposed to be no passage at all, and took two days to find their way out—*Krait* slowly crept towards their final base. On 26th August they sighted North West Cape, the western protective arm of Exmouth Gulf.

3

WITH *KRAIT* TO SINGAPORE

EXMOUTH GULF IS A GREAT, BARREN INLET TWENTY-FIVE miles wide on the north-western corner of Australia. Facing north, it provides admirable shelter from the prevailing trade winds and by the autumn of 1943 had become an advanced American submarine base. It looked good to Ivan Lyon and his men after three weeks spent dodging the reefs and tide-rips of the Timor Sea. Three days of American hospitality soon had them in fighting form. *Krait*'s low freeboard must have been another inch deeper in the water with all the presents and extra rations showered on them. They weighed anchor at ten o'clock in the morning of September 1 and went alongside the tanker S.S. *Ondina* to take on their final load of oil and water.

That day, Lyon sent a last guarded letter home saying that for a Gordon Highlander he led a very queer life of the "close to nature" variety. He told his parents that he was burnt so black and had become so leathery that it would take a lot of peace-time living to return him to his comfortable self. He added wryly that his adventures in the war would set him up afterwards as a first-class club bore and wished he could say something of them, which was, of course, not possible. He ended wistfully that if only his wife and son were there, he would be a very happy chap.

At half past five they cast off, with everything shipshape and ready for sea. Exactly one minute later, the shaft extension piece on the engine broke. Paddy McDowell's imprecations shook the engine room more than the broken shaft, but even his loving care could not achieve the impossible. *Krait* was immobilised and had to anchor. It looked as if the whole expedition would have to be called off. Only a long tow down to Fremantle and a week in the dockyards would put the damage right and by that time their time-table would start to overlap the monsoon. Lyon and Davidson were drafting the unpleasant wireless messages telling of their plight when, three hours later, the U.S.S. *Chanticleer*, the submarine-repair ship, entered the bay. This was too good to be true. Lyon had himself rowed across in the dinghy, and in no time *Chanticleer* sent a motorboat to tow *Krait* alongside. The broken shaft was taken out and by the following morning brazed together again, although the American mechanics insisted that it was only a temporary job and might perhaps get them back to Fremantle for a proper replacement.

Lyon, who had come to trust Paddy McDowell completely, asked him what he thought. "I think it will hold," the tough old Scot replied imperturbably—and that with 4000 miles ahead of them in enemy waters and no spare. Lyon did not hesitate. At two o'clock in the afternoon of September 2 they put to sea—and three hours later nearly foundered.

As they cleared North West Cape, the full force of the wind hit them. With a wicked tide-rip running, *Krait* was beam on to the Force 7 westerly seas. They knew she could roll, but this was outside all their previous experience. Badly overloaded, she lurched drunkenly from side to side, with great green seas pouring inboard and crashing on the afterdeck. The wheelhouse looked like the conning tower of a submarine, completely awash. The hatches to the cabin and the engine room were battened down, but the men off watch in the cramped space under the awning had to hang on for their lives to the nearest stanchion, often waist-deep in swirling water.

It seemed as if one particularly large wave had finally put them under. Nothing of *Krait* was visible forward of the wheelhouse. She trembled, shuddered, almost on her beam ends, and then, just as it seemed as if they were going down, slowly shook herself free. Lyon himself was at the helm and slowly, with the help of Carse, managed to fight *Krait* round to port, head on to the murderous sea. For the faithful Morris, clinging desperately to the rails by the engine house, it was the worst moment of the whole voyage. The tough Welsh miner had really thought that his last moment had come.

Within an hour they were out of the coastal tide-rip and in relatively calmer water. Course was once more set to the north.

The third day out, with only a gentle swell, white

cloud flecks in the blue sky and a warm breeze presaging the hot days that lay ahead, Lyon called the crew together under the awning: "It's time you knew where we are really going," he told them. "It is not Surabaya, it's Singapore. I am sorry I couldn't tell you before, but we had to keep it completely dark for security reasons."

Singapore—more than a thousand miles inside the new Japanese empire—was a very different proposition from Surabaya, just round the corner once they were through the Lombok Straits, but the men were absolutely exhilarated at the prospect. This was something really worth doing. They slapped each other on the back, yippee'd, good-oh'd, and pranced around like schoolboys. Perhaps only Morris realised the implications of what lay ahead of them. He thought of the maze of islands he and Lyon had traversed in the early disastrous months of 1942 and then imagined their little craft trying to force the same waters entirely under Japanese control. For once, his sunny Welsh temperament could not respond. But he knew his Lyon. If anyone could get away with such a piece of sheer audacity, this was the man.

Later that day they started blackening themselves with the skin dye they had brought with them. It was a sticky, evil-smelling mixture, thinned with spirit. It stuck to everything better than it did to their own bodies. They had to leave white rings round their eyes because of the spirit and another white patch round their private parts, although the native *sarongs* they donned put that right. Sweat, water, and oil brought it off again, and however often they applied the dye, they never presented anything better than a curiously mottled appearance. It might serve to confuse the Japanese and natives from a distance, but, close to, the blue eyes of most of the party would give them away.

If challenged, the plan was for Jones, Berryman, and Huston, the three darkest of them, to run on to the foredeck, gesticulating innocently and pointing at the Japanese flag they were going to hoist at the stern. If that did not work, massed gunfire from the rest of the crew under the awning and the trick with the dinghy were the only resources left. None of the others would bear close scrutiny. McDowell looked like a stringy fakir, Carse vaguely Burmese, and Lyon might pass under a cursory glance for a Malay—except for those green eyes. But Poppa Falls was definitely ginger and Young quite fair and if they put the dye in their hair it stood up as if electrified, with patches of the original colour showing through where the scalp sweated. The only real defence was somehow to dodge all shipping.

Carse, his logbook looking more like a Scotland Yard fingerprint record with its black smudges, thought little of the experiment: "It proved a rank failure," he wrote, "more black everywhere than on the person after an hour or two. The crew now resemble blackamoors. A more desperate looking crowd I have never seen. The sea remains calm and glory be praised the scattered clouds of this morning are becoming more and more numerous, showing every indication of poor to bad visibility for the day of days, or rather night of nights."

He was thinking four days ahead to the dangerous passage of the closely guarded straits between the islands of Lombok and Bali, the gantlet *Krait* would have to run to break through into the South China Sea. The following day, the sixth, with the sky clouding up nicely, they hauled down their blue ensign and hoisted in its place the poached egg of Japan. The flag they had brought with them was far too clean and new for its purpose, so they scuffed it round the deck with their feet until it looked sufficiently grubby and weather-beaten. Paddy McDowell also switched his engine over to the silencer and the powerful chug-chug-chug of the exhaust died away to a reassuring purr. It cut a little off their speed and they never reached seven knots again.

With the look-outs' eyes peeled for enemy aircraft, they held course to the north. The Admiralty pilot book for the eastern archipelago informed them that at this time of year weather conditions would be hazy, with visibility down to 6000 yards, but to their consternation the weather during the seventh was as bright, clear, and sunny as a spring day. The eighth dawned the same, and, to add to their troubles, the engine started coughing on a faulty feed pipe, but this was repaired during the morning.

They were now well within range of Japanese air patrols, and they knew there was a large air base at Den Pasar on Bali. Shortly after midday they sighted the mountain peaks of Lombok and Bali to the north.

They needed night for the dash through the straits between them, so they throttled down to four knots and even spent a couple of hours going back on their tracks to gain time. After they had turned again in the late afternoon they passed within twenty feet of a large floating log, surrounded by a school of huge sharks which seemed to be trying to bite it. It was not a pleasant sight and considerably doused their spirits. It was not only Japanese air and naval patrol craft they had to fear.

By dusk, the massive island volcanoes, Gunong Agoeng, 10,000 feet on Bali, and Gunong Rindjani, 12,000 feet on Lombok, seemed to fill half the sky. Nusa Besar Island, in the middle of the entrance to the straits, was about fourteen miles distant. As the light faded, a powerful searchlight started to sweep from the high land on the south-eastern corner of Bali off their port bow.

Lyon and Davidson were in the wheelhouse with Ted Carse. "What do you think, Don? Can we make it?" Lyon asked. Davidson gave a slight shrug of his shoulders. Carse had been watching the sweep of the light intently. "If we keep well over to the Lombok side," he said, "the flash should pass over the top of our mast. We are so low in the water that I think we shall be below their horizon." Paddy McDowell was told to subject his faulty bearing to maximum revolutions, a glorious six and a half knots, and, heading slightly to the north-east, *Krait* started to force the fifty-mile passage.

Misled again by the pilot book, they had underestimated the southerly tidal set in the narrows. Once a day the whole of the Java Sea tries to pour through this narrow funnel into the Indian Ocean, and they had caught this tremendous rip at its height. By 9 o'clock they were barely abeam of Nusa Besar Island. An hour later, as a fixed steady light became visible on its highest point, probably an observation post, they were barely a mile further ahead. At eleven o'clock they had actually lost ground and were back in the same position as they had been two hours earlier. The tide was running faster than the straining diesel could push the overloaded craft.

Between midnight and four in the morning they made about six miles. They had passed innumerable flickering lights, some of which might be bush-clearing fires, but several of which looked like the headlights of motor cars. They had assumed Nusa Besar to be uninhabited—it had been, under the Dutch—but there was so much activity that they were thankful they had not carried out their original intention of lying up under its lee during the day and attempting the passage on the second night.

With every man on look-out, they peered into the darkness. Tired eyes can play curious tricks. Once, Lyon, who seemed to have a cat's vision at night, thought he saw a cruiser closing them, with three masts and a huge bow wave. After a few tense minutes, with arms at the ready, the bow wave resolved itself into a tide-rip and the masts into three tall trees on the top of a distant hill. Another naval patrol craft seen through their night-glasses turned out to be a sailing junk, beating laboriously against the current.

Although *Krait* was taking several minutes to thump through the worst of the tide-rips, the force of the current was now slackening, and Carse was reasonably sanguine about their being safely clear by the morning.

Their hopes were rudely shattered. As dawn broke they were still in the northern narrows, with Nusa Besar just visible astern. Daybreak was so spectacular that for a moment they forgot their danger. As the sun struck the top of the towering volcano, Gunong Agoeng, on Bali and the morning mists started to roll down the sides, the light caught the prismatic colours on the pinnacles and outcrops, cascading down, like a torch shone on mosaic. As the clouds cleared, the coast was left clear with perfect visibility. To the east, on the Lombok side, a merciful haze persisted, which should shield them from being sighted from Ampenan, the only known Japanese base in the area.

There was nothing for it but to hold a steady course and hope for the best. Back under the awning, Morris, Marsh, Falls, and Berryman, suddenly finding their voices after the breath-taking beauty of the dawn, started to grumble good-humouredly about the planning which had placed them so utterly exposed and defenceless in full view of the enemy coast. But they were more interested in watching Andrew Crilly frying his pancakes and brewing up the tea. No one panicked and they were ready for anything. "This was the first opportunity to judge the crew under seemingly hazardous conditions," Lyon wrote later in his report. "Their complete calm was most encouraging."

Apart from sighting a few coastal sailing *prahus*, no alarm was raised. At ten in the morning Carse wrote in his log: "Fixed position 8° 5′ South, 115° 55′ East. Thank Christ we are through the Strait, steering for Sekala, 68 miles distant. After a clear early morning the haze now at 1020 is increasing, although the island of Bali is still clearly visible. Lombok is almost totally obscured. . . . This war is certainly hard on the nervous system."

If all went well the next part of their journey should be less eventful. Keeping to the east of the Kangean Islands, north of the Lombok Straits, the plan was to turn north-west, skirting the coast of Borneo, and then strike across to the Lingga Archipelago, the most southerly group of the maze of islands extending up to Singapore.

On the tenth, the day after they had cleared Lombok, Ted Carse's log was much more cheerful and discursive: "The morale of the crew is excellent. Corporal Crilly is doing a marvellous job in making all meals tasty in spite of bad weather and worse conditions. . . . By dark tonight we will be across the main shipping routes from Surabaya and Batavia to Balik Papan, Timor and all ports using the Macassar Strait. Our look-outs are particularly keen and so far have always sighted any objects long before we could possibly be seen by them. We have ample supplies of everything needed except water, which is rationed to three cups of tea a day and a water bottle every three days. Most of them seem to have no difficulty in this but I have been praying for a good shower of rain ever since the days have become hot. In latitude 5° South, with the sun only 5° North, its heat as close to the water as we are is terrific. The decks become too hot to stand on in bare feet. To counteract this, our freeboard is so little that with even a calm sea our waist is continually awash.

"Our engineer, Leading Stoker McDowell, has been invaluable. He has worked day and night training crew and operatives to help him in his duties and to be able to operate the engine should anything happen to him, as well as tending and servicing the engine. In fact he looks after the engine better and treats it more carefully than a mother would a baby. No matter how long the hours, he works away, stopping troubles before they develop and always cheerful and happy. No man could be better suited to the job than he is.

"Lieutenant Page has one fault. He is always trying to doctor someone up. His latest suggestion is to put all hands on a course of Doctor Bland's pills. For the sake of their health he puts it, but I think that it is to study their reactions while undergoing the said course.

"The success which has so far attended our efforts may be likely to create over-confidence in the crew; but they are so well chosen and so keen that I do not think this very likely.

"Most of the dye has washed off by now and we all resemble studies in black and white. This is our ninth day out and so far not one case of sickness reported. A few are showing the signs of barked shins, due to collisions with tins in the dark of night. At the present the others are discussing iced beer and cigarettes, which can't be got nearer than Australia, so I suppose I had better join them."

The days and nights settled down to a routine. Lyon, Davidson, and Carse took their turn at the wheel, alternating with Cobber Cain and Morris, who would have to stand watch at the helm during the long fortnight once the operatives had been launched for the attack on Singapore. Young was below at his wireless set, taking down weather and news reports, but more often than not tuning in to music programmes, which came drifting up through the hatch to entertain the members of the crew off watch. Otherwise they congregated under the awning aft, crowded with its hammocks slung from the roof and the four mattresses laid out on the deckhouse of the engine room.

Most evenings Morris and Crilly, the only two army men among the crew, used to sit together with their knees up, humming duets, in which the others would sometimes join. Morris, with his clear Welsh tenor and inexhaustible repertoire, was the song-bird of the party. Cheerful, imperturbable, ready to lend his hand to anything, his sturdy courage was a splendid example to the younger members of the crew.

Everyone was under strain, and sleep was largely a matter of uneasy catnapping, waking fully alert to seize a gun at the slightest touch of hand on shoulder. Morris was the barometer by which they set their morning mood. An early morning start was nothing to a man from the Welsh mining valleys. He was always up the first, and if he was singing "O Sole Mio" or a Gilbert and Sullivan ballad, they knew all was right with the world. Modern songs indicated a heavy swell and likely storms, but if he was singing "Men of Harlech" or "The British Grenadiers," then danger was afoot.

The practical joker of the party was still Marsh. This big, jocular, likeable grizzly bear was always up to some prank or other: hiding people's eating utensils, rolling up their blankets in some inaccessible position, tripping them up when they were not looking, but always ready to be wrestled to the deck and have the breath beaten out of him by his outraged victims. He never tangled with Falls, the easy-going giant with the magnificent physique, as Falls was not a man to provoke too far; nor with Cobber Cain, the vast, good-humoured bosun's mate, who kept *Krait* shipshape.

Sometimes Lyon and Davidson would come aft, Davidson to yarn about his farming and jungle days and Lyon to talk more quietly about his lone canoe trips or the job that lay ahead. Page was the junior officer of the expedition and was a little over-shadowed by his three seniors, although he went quietly about his work, spreading an indefinable air of confidence. The Australians in the crew swore by him. He was of their own stock and a man of natural intelligence, authority, and dignity, for whom they would have done anything. Ted Carse, with his weather-beaten monkey face, was more saturnine and mixed with the others less. He did not have the robust good health and vitality of the rest of them and his world was the wheelhouse, plotting the course of this ramshackle, decrepit craft through the maze of currents and the empty seas which would bring them to their destination.

The other dedicated man was Paddy McDowell. He had got to know every square inch of his engine so well that he needed no light down in the broiling heat. He could run his hands over the bearings in the dark and when, as a concession, he let Marsh take over from time to time so that he could take a spell on deck, the faintest change of note in the diesel, imperceptible to normal ears, would send him scurrying below again. Gaunt and tireless, he was far older than anyone else on board, over fifty, and the youngsters treated him as a benevolent uncle, listening awe-struck in his rare relaxed moments to his heroic accounts of consumption in all the bars of Australia of the cold, clear beer he craved.

By now there was no beer left aboard. What little there had been in the way of parting presents had long since been drunk, the bottles carefully smashed as they dropped them overboard, to leave no trace. They took the same precautions with everything else. The labels off the food tins were carefully burnt, the tins themselves punctured to ensure that they would sink without trace. Some cigarettes they did have, although smoking was strictly forbidden on deck at any time and it was a question of snatching a few quick puffs down in the engine room or perhaps in the forward cabin with Young.

This was particularly hard on Morris, who had been a heavy smoker, but he came into his reward. A rum ration was issued every evening, not ceremoniously served round by measured tot as in the Navy, but splashed into willing mugs until the bottle was empty. Morris simply could not develop a taste for it. He tried it neat, he tried it watered down, he tried it sweetened, and only regretted later that he had not tried mixing it with the lime juice which was always available to keep down scabies. Finally he arranged that his ration should be kept in the bottle, and by the time they returned to Exmouth Gulf he had hoarded four handsome quart flagons. He found himself the most popular man in the American submarine base, where every ship was "dry." Refusing offers of five pounds in hard cash for each bottle, he declined to exchange it on any but a barter basis and ended up with three sack-loads of American cigarettes, which made up for all his previous privations.

Sarongs and bare feet had become second nature to them. In training for the task ahead, they had learned to do without such marks of Western civilisation as toilet paper. They scrubbed their teeth in salt water and accustomed themselves to think of every normal act in terms of the clues it might provide to an observant enemy. Nothing was to be left to chance.

Life was comparatively easy. In spite of the strain, particularly to the eyes, of constant watches and look-outs, no one started to get edgy and tempers remained good. It was Andy Crilly, cramped into his galley under the awning aft, who let off steam for all of them. In many ways he had the hardest job of all, and he did it magnificently. Whatever the weather, there was always a cup of steaming tea in the morning for everyone and two good mugs of stew a day. The dehydrated food took a lot of preparing. The vegetables and meat had to be soaked for hours before they were fit for human consumption, and whenever there was a bit of a sea running his pots and pans would slide from one end to the other of the stove. He would grab them just as they were about to topple overboard, cursing and blasting at the top of his voice, but never failing to come up with something when mealtime was due. Their original store of bread had long since been eaten, and when they started getting tired of hard biscuits, he began to produce pancakes. There were always tinned pork sausages and citrus fruits to vary the menu and he never once let them down.

They sighted the Borneo coast off Tanjong Puting, and Carse's log notes of the off-shore islands marked their progress: Tanjong Sambar, Pelapsis, Nasa Tiga, and Penebangan. They sighted a number of junks and native craft, but none of them altered course to intercept them, and if anyone looked as if they were going to pass too near, *Krait* altered course herself to clear them.

On two or three occasions, Lyon called the other five operatives, Davidson, Page, Falls, Huston, and Jones, together to run through their plans and pore over the charts of the Rhio Archipelago, so that each pair knew their duty and courses by heart. Marsh and Berryman were the first reserves should anything happen to one of the others, so they were fully briefed as well. Lyon had made up his mind that the canoes would be disembarked at Pulau Durian, whence he and Morris had directed the escape routes in that disastrous spring of 1942. He knew every inch of the way between there and Singapore.

By the fourteenth they were standing away from Borneo on the last lap of their sea journey. That evening Carse made another of his revealing log entries: "A heavy cloud bank surmounted by mare's tails is rising astern. It might presage a fairly heavy blow. No rain so far. I can visualise a small nudist colony when it does come and bad luck for the man at the wheel. Summing up this afternoon, I decided we had seven more really dangerous days with the ship. Namely, to-day and tomorrow, dropping and picking up operatives, two days for this passage on return and, last but not least, THE STRAIT. If we survive the next two days the operation should be carried out successfully and then for our return journey. All the ship's company are in the best of health and spirits and are thoroughly enjoying the trip. So far we have experienced the most wonderful weather. Right from Cairns we had a following wind and sea (these are the conditions in which the ship behaves best) and no really bad weather. But the last three days we have seen no flying fish at all. This seems rather remarkable in these waters. One solitary turtle was seen to-day and countless jellyfish.

"The main topic of conversation these days is of course the job in hand. Fortune so far has been very kind to us and providing she still remains kind we will be eating dinner in Australia this day next month.

"The sailing vessels seen this morning were all

apparently engaged in the coastal trade along the coast of Borneo, as we have seen none since we started across the Karimata Strait. By what we have so far seen it seems quite logical that we can get back again the same way, as by the time we start our return trip the tumult and shouting should have died. It seems peculiar that we should be cruising at our leisure through these seas with no sign of challenges, but there is a feeling of anxiety all the same. This is definitely not the same as the Lombok type but is there all the same. Each day as the sun goes down, I mutter a heartfelt 'Thank God.' "

The next day they sighted a junk on a converging course and *Krait*'s labouring engine was unable to shake her off. "The fact that we can't leave a junk behind, although she is beating slightly to windward, is causing quite a little merriment," Carse commented. The two ships remained within sight of each other most of the day, but as the wind shifted during the afternoon, *Krait* started to draw ahead, without any sign of suspicious activity on the junk. Just to make sure, everyone had rubbed on another coat of their foul-smelling, sticky dye and Carse's logbook was covered again with his smudged fingerprints. There was also a more worrying note: "My eyes have been giving trouble lately," he wrote. "I can't read the sextant now by artificial light and this will mean working by sun and dead reckoning. Sun sights at present are rather unsatisfactory. Probably with a fortnight's rest away from this constant glare, they will improve sufficiently for the run home. I sincerely hope so."

As day broke on September 16 they were approaching the Temiang Strait, one of the eastern outlets of the group of islands of the Lingga and Rhio archipelagoes, which stud the South China Sea between Singapore and Sumatra. They were now within a hundred miles of their target. Arms were inspected, their camouflage renewed, and every man, except the look-outs, told to remain under the awning with the minimum of movement.

Soon Sebanga Island was abeam to port, with the 3000-foot peak of Lingga Island plainly visible behind it. After their week in the open sea, these confined waters spelt new danger. From now on they would never be out of sight of land, and they could expect Japanese patrol activities to increase with each mile they approached nearer to their goal. At ten o'clock that morning they saw their first aircraft, apparently heading north for Singapore on a steady course, and then two sailing ships coming down the Strait towards them. One was a European-type yacht, probably captured at the fall of Singapore, but they both ignored *Krait* and, to everyone's delight, a cloud bank started building up from Sumatra, reducing visibility drastically and threatening a violent storm. The heavy black cloud formations came boiling up from the west, blotting out the sky. Lyon, Davidson, and Morris had seen this phenomenon before. It heralded a dreaded "Sumatra," a violent cyclonic storm which has wise seamen running for harbour. *Krait* had weathered conditions as bad when clearing Exmouth Gulf and if they could hold course they might be able to get through the Strait without detection.

Suddenly Davidson gave the order for action stations, each man taking up his Sten or Bren gun and going to his loophole post under the awning. Not 400 yards ahead, a 10,000-ton freighter emerged from the murk on their port side and cut across their bows. They reduced speed immediately, but the ship held on course and gave no evidence of having sighted them. Minutes later the storm struck and everything was blotted out. The wind hit *Krait* as if she had collided head on with a solid rock. The sea was lashed in-board, lifting spindrift twenty or thirty feet high. Then came the torrential rain lasting nearly three quarters of an hour.

The more inexperienced members of the crew had been warned what to expect, and once the first shock was over, busied themselves carrying a large sail for-ward to catch the precious fresh water. Hanging on grimly to rails and stanchions, they ferried every con-tainer they possessed past the wheelhouse to fill up the water tanks. Drenched, shouting, and happy, revelling in their first bath for a fortnight, the tension of half an hour earlier was completely forgotten.

The storm cleared as quickly as it had come, and they found that they were through the Strait and al-ready north of Pompong Island, the first Lyon had decided to reconnoitre as their rear base for the pick-up and get-away. They were now in the almost land-girt sea, some 60 miles from east to west and 150 miles from north to south, which lies between the coast of

Sumatra and the convex sweep of the islands of the Rhio and Lingga archipelagoes. To the north, within a score of miles of Singapore, the islands curve round towards Sumatra to form a natural barrier, with only half a dozen narrow channels between them. *Krait* had avoided the wide and well-guarded Singapore Straits, which lead into the port from the east, but was safely within the inner barrier to the south. Her outward task was largely done. Almost any of the islands in the northern part of this inland sea were within canoe range of their target.

They run very much to a pattern. Humps of dark-green jungle, heavy with ficus palm and knotted undergrowth, vibrate in the heat haze, with mud flats and mangrove swamp on the shore, interspersed with rocky outcrops and small sandy beaches. Most of the inhabitants live in fishing villages, either built on stilts along the shoreline or clustered on some rare stretch of level land with a clearing for their primitive agriculture behind. Except for the occasional plantation, everything else is jungle, teeming with animal life. If they chose their hides carefully, the canoe teams were unlikely to be discovered even by the occasional hunter. The villagers are nearly all fishermen, their means of communication the *kolek* and the *prahu*. To these men *Krait* would be an object of no interest, provided her movements were not suspicious. But the canoes—that was another matter. They were unlike anything to be found in these waters and the merest sight of one of them would cause a buzz of *kampong* gossip.

Reducing speed, *Krait* turned south and slowly ran past Pompong Island. There seemed far too many native huts and fishing stakes along the shores for comfort and as they stood in to round a point they had another bad scare. Carse suddenly sighted a long straight mast with crosstrees about a mile and a half away, its structure unmistakeably that of a naval patrol craft. Clamping on full speed and swinging the helm over, he turned through 180 degrees and sent little Berryman, with his keen eyes, scurrying up *Krait*'s own mast to report.

The look-out soon had reassuring news. Only the mast was visible sticking out of the water and it must belong to a wreck. *Krait* turned again and as they sailed past Lyon recognised it. It was all that was left of H.M.S. *Kuala,* the British gunboat which had been sunk off Pompong in the tragic days of February 1942, with its load of refugees, whom he had subsequently ferried over to Sumatra and safety. "Ghost Island" had certainly lived up to its name.

Krait then stood over to the eastwards to see if Bengku Island offered any better shelter, but they found it surrounded by a seemingly impassable reef. They launched the dinghy to take soundings, and Davidson was just about to cast off when they heard the sound of an aircraft. It was coming in so low that for a moment they could not see it. With quick presence of mind, Lyon snatched up one of the conical coolie straw hats they were carrying on board, tossed it down to Davidson, quickly donned one himself, and as the plane roared over at not more than a hundred feet, looked up at it and waved in the most natural manner in the world. He could actually see the Japanese pilot looking down at them. He gave no sign of surprise, continued straight on, and was soon out of sight. It had been a bad moment. Lyon blew out his cheeks in relief and blessed the foresight which had made him have everyone blacken themselves with the dye as soon as the storm was over. Curious as they looked, it obviously worked.

Bengku proved useless, and towards evening they moved back to Pompong, where they had spotted one sheltered and uninhabited bay. They christened it Fisherman's Bay and dropped anchor for the night. The four officers held a conference. In spite of the scares of the day, Lyon had made up his mind that patrol activity was limited and that the best thing for *Krait* to do was to cruise gently northwards and then strike west to Pulau Durian, to arrive at dusk the following day.

In case the plane or any of the ships should have reported their presence, they decided to unstep the mast, thus altering their outline and giving *Krait* such a low silhouette that she would be even more difficult to spot. They were a little unhappy about the operation in the dark, and the mast came down with a thunderous crash on the wheelhouse, in spite of the last minute effort of Huston to stop it. Davidson shouted at him to stand clear, otherwise he might have been badly hurt. After they had cleared away the debris, they started hauling out the folded canoes and operational stores from the forward hold, which soon littered the deck. Most native craft carried a large amount of deck cargo and there was no reason to suppose that this would excite suspicion.

Later that evening, two searchlights opened up from the south, their beams weaving a circular pattern as they criss-crossed, lighting up the trees on Pompong and the surrounding sea. The islands of the Lingga Archipelago had been little frequented when Lyon had last seen them and this was clearly something new. In the small hours came the unmistakeable sound of aero engines being revved up. This could only mean that the Japanese had set up a patrol base of some sort, probably of float planes, to scour the narrow passages and inlets between the islands surrounding Singapore. The base could not be far away either. Davidson suggested excitedly that they should launch their first attack straight away, take two of the folboats in the direction of the engine noises, and sabotage as many of the planes as they could. Lyon calmed him down. There would be no point in giving away their presence at such an early juncture and the limpet mines were destined for bigger game.

The plan was to remain at Pompong until at least mid-day, as there were only thirty miles to cover to Pulau Durian and they wanted to be able to go straight there without loitering too much on the way. At dawn, to confirm their suspicions of the night, two float planes flew over. Their anchorage was obviously unhealthy. Then, towards nine o'clock, a *kolek* with three natives in it rounded the point and made towards them. This was too much to risk. They could not afford to start *kampong* gossip at this stage, so they quickly weighed anchor and moved out towards the north.

They had several hours to kill and Lyon decided that the best tactics would be to cruise slowly up the western coast of the islands in the general direction of Singapore, ready to duck into one of the narrow passages or inlets if they sighted anything likely to take an interest in them. Rounding Sabang Besar, with a long string of fishing huts along its shores, they turned eastwards towards Galang Baru, with Lyon, Davidson, and Carse in the wheelhouse and everyone else under cover, relying on the harmless and battered appearance of *Krait* to avoid challenge.

As they closed the island, they could see what appeared to be a rubber planter's bungalow set amongst the dark-green foliage. When they came within two miles, Lyon suddenly stiffened. There was another building in the trees behind and further up the hill, an unmistakeable observation tower. They had run straight into real trouble. Lyon swung the engine-room telegraph to full speed ahead so that they would not appear to be loitering aimlessly, and changed course due north again. With luck the look-outs would assume that the dirty little ship was on its way from Sumatra to Singapore. No challenge came, no shots were fired, no patrol boat put out in their direction, but the observation tower was fiendishly well sited. It remained clearly visible astern for miles, and the one thing they could not risk was the further turn of course to the west which would take them to Pulau Durian. That would have looked really suspicious. They were now moving away from their destination and it would soon be impossible for them to get back to Pulau Durian with any hope of dropping the operatives and clearing it again during the night.

At such a crisis Lyon was at his best. Coolly, he changed his entire dispositions. They must hold course to the north and look for a new forward base.

"I don't know how the day is going to end," Carse was writing in his log, voicing the feelings of them all. "We have been zig-zagging and zig-zagging all day long from one deserted spot to another, only to find that we are approaching a worse one. Out of the frying pan into the fire would be appropriate, but it does the system no good. We have been looking for a place to anchor but the population is against us. As long as we keep moving, no matter how aimlessly, we don't seem to excite suspicion, but I don't think we could do it for long. We are within about 30 odd miles of Singapore and still getting closer by means of a staggered course, waiting and praying for dark. No lovers ever longed for darkness as we do, although it will probably show us the lights of Singapore. One thing about it is that we should be able to pick up all searchlights and observation post positions guarding the city. The one we saw is guarding Dempu Strait and in our usual inconsequent way, we approached it on a more or less innocent course, so probably were only given a passing glance. Hope so anyway. The sky is still overcast, wind and sea calm.

"This O.P. takes away one of our possible get-aways and taken in conjunction with the seaplane base, limits us to the Merredong and Temiang Straits. As we came through Temiang, scanning the shores closely and saw only native habitations, I am hoping to be able to use that tomorrow and also on our return."

Lyon had always hoped that *Krait* would be able to lie up in some deep cove, camouflaged with branches against the shore, to await the return of the attack party. This plan had now been abandoned. No suitable cover had been found, and in the eighteen months since he was last in these waters, the Japanese had clearly organised extensive patrol activity. He would have to take the risk of sending *Krait* on an innocent-appearing run to Borneo, returning for the rendez-vous. She was safer in the uninhabited sea lanes, off the main shipping routes, than in this congested litter of islands.

At four o'clock in the afternoon they passed along the small island of Panjang. A dark-green hump of hill and jungle, it appeared entirely uninhabited and offered several good beaches and sandy coves. Lyon made up his mind at once. This would be the base for the canoes, but they dare not land and reconnoitre in daylight, still within view of the observation post on Galang Baru, so they carried on northwards towards the Bulan Strait approach to Singapore to waste the three remaining hours of daylight.

Off Tanjong Klingking, about five miles north of Panjang, they stood more than a little wearily to action stations as what appeared to be a patrol craft put out from a *kampong* about three miles away. *Krait* altered course warily, and after a few minutes it was clear that the launch was paying no attention to them, but was crowded with natives in blue clothing and was probably an inter-island ferry.

Everyone was distinctly jittery by now. As the Strait narrowed and dusk began to fall, they sighted what looked like another patrol craft and stood to arms again. It turned out to be a large fishing *pagar*, a sort of houseboat permanently moored above a set of native fishing nets.

It would be half past seven before it was dark enough for them to turn about. As the tropical night fell, a diffused glow seemed to fill the northern sky, even individual specks of light appeared. Lyon grabbed Davidson by the elbow. "There she is, Donald," he said. They were looking at the reflection of the lights of Singapore, twinkling a mere twenty-two miles ahead. They called the rest of the crew up into the bows. There was no mistaking the elation in Lyon's usually calm voice as he told them what they were looking at. The tension suddenly seemed to lift. The voyage was half over, they were safe, and they now knew the full extent of what was required of them. Slapping each other on the back, pointing, wrestling, panting in their excitement, it was several minutes before they took up their stations again.

Ivan Lyon stood off to one side, taking no part in the horse-play. His dream was on the way to being fulfilled. The frustrated subaltern who had so loathed orthodox soldiering was about to prove himself. He had devised this whole daring plan, recruited and trained the men, and brought them within a score of miles of their goal. So skilled were they that the actual attack seemed the easiest part of the expedition. The Japanese would never be expecting enemy forces to debouch from this direction and they stood an excellent chance of escaping undetected.

He thought of Willy Graham, his C.O. in the Gordons, of Major Lees and his wife, who had been so kind to Gaby, of the little bungalow in which they had lived during their marriage, and of Gaby and Clive . . . far away in Tokyo in some vile internment camp. He thought again of the humiliation of the days of defeat– By God, the Japanese were going to pay for it!

Elsewhere in the world, on that September evening, the Western allies were struggling to keep their Salerno beachhead, the Germans had reoccupied Rome, but the Italian Navy lay under the guns of Malta and Gibraltar; the Yugoslav guerrillas had broken through to the Dalmatian coast; the Russians were recapturing Smolensk and the Kuban Delta opposite the Crimea; Allied bombers had destroyed Hamburg and were pounding Berlin; in Burma, American engineers were just starting work on the new Ledo Road into China; far to the east, General MacArthur was counter-attacking in New Guinea and was pushing up into the Solomons. But the Allied "invasion force" cruising warily within sight of Singapore consisted of a major in the Gordon Highlanders, two lieutenants in the Royal Naval Volunteer Reserve, a lieutenant in the Australian Army, and exactly ten assorted other ranks. There was not another Allied soldier in arms within two thousand miles of them. In the stinking jungles of

Siam, the army Lyon had been ordered to leave a year and a half earlier was dying in its hundreds on the infamous railway the Japanese were forcing them to build into Siam.

Lyon whispered an order and Carse turned *Krait* round for her run back to Panjang. They started to get out the rest of the attack stores on the forward deck. Lyon, Davidson, and Page watched their every move to make sure that there was no last-minute confusion, while Carse's bad eyes peered ahead to con their position.

"As we turned, we noticed a searchlight coming from the Galang Baru O.P.," he wrote later in his log. "Then a violent rain squall accompanied by heavy, gusty winds struck us, obscuring everything. Suddenly out of the darkness ahead, our fishing *pagar* showed a lovely bright light. As we were at that time surrounded by reefs, with a strong ebb tide and no vision, it appeared God sent. If we return from this trip I am thinking of setting up a monument to their glory."

They arrived off Panjang at ten o'clock and anchored, but the sea was too rough and the wind too high to risk landing. At midnight the weather showed no signs of abating, so they weighed anchor to see if they could find a lee shore on the opposite side of the island. No sooner had they got under way than the wind dropped. They moved inshore again and Davidson and Jones paddled to the beach in the dinghy to reconnoitre. Within half an hour Jones was back, to say that the beach was perfect for the purpose.

The crew had practised transporting the canoes and

loading the stores so often that they could do it blindfold. Quickly Lyon ran through the final check: arms, knives, charts, binoculars, rations and water for a month, protective clothing, and, last but not least, the mines and spares that went with them. *Krait's* freeboard was so low that loading the dinghy presented no difficulty. Paddy McDowell came up from the engine room, and Young from his wireless set, to see them off. Then, just as the dinghy was on its last trip came the unmistakeable thud of an auxiliary motor.

Everyone froze, not uttering a whisper. Not fifty yards out to sea, the outlines of a junk crept slowly past them. She did not appear to sight *Krait* at all, which was entirely likely, as her low, dark silhouette must have been almost invisible against the trees of the island. The junk carried on her course to the north, but from then on no one spoke above a hoarse whisper. It was now half past four in the morning. Morris shouldered his way forward and leant over to shake Lyon by the hand: "The very best of luck, sir, and may we be seeing you again soon," he said. "Thank you, Morris, I hope so indeed," replied Lyon to his oldest companion.

The others were being more jocular in their farewells. "Put one down for me, Happy," said Mostyn Berryman to his constant wrestling companion, Huston. "The best of luck, Arty," said Biffo Marsh, and even Paddy McDowell joined in: "Look after yourself, Poppa," he said to Falls, "and come back to Daddy." The moment told worst on Marsh and Berryman. As the two reserve operatives, they had hoped desperately to take part in the final attack. But the other three bowmen were all fit and the die was cast.

Light-hearted as it all was, those left on *Krait* had the nagging thought that they might be seeing their six companions for the last time. The pick-up was to be at Pompong after dusk on October 1. This would avoid the Galang Baru observation post and mean that they could cut straight to the east through the Temiang Strait and head for home. If anything went wrong, *Krait* was not to wait beyond the rendez-vous date, but to return to Exmouth Gulf without the operatives. There was no point in risking the whole party, and Lyon was confident that if the six of them survived they would be able to capture a junk and find their own way home.

Krait and the shore party lost sight of each other in a matter of seconds. Carse ordered the anchor weighed, and the blur of Panjang quickly disappeared behind them as he set course first to the south-west to stand well out from the dangerous observation post and then, as dawn broke, turned south-east and ran for the Temiang Strait and Borneo.

4

TED CARSE'S LOG

"KRAIT" WAS LEFT WITH A MUCH REDUCED AND RATHER subdued little company for the nerve-wracking fortnight that lay ahead. The taciturn Carse was now in command and with him were Cain, Marsh, Berryman, Morris, and Crilly, with Young still on his wireless watch and Paddy McDowell down in the engine room. In some ways theirs was the harder part to bear. The three canoe crews would be holing up by day and paddling their blacked-out folboats towards Singapore by night, with every hope of escaping detection, except during the actual attack. *Krait*, with her reduced firepower, would be cruising day and night in the dangerous waters of the South China seas, with only half as many men on deck to defend her should she run into trouble.

As day broke after leaving Panjang, they were only halfway between Petong and Abang Besar islands, still well within the island screen of the Rhio and Lingga archipelagoes. Astern, the small lighthouses on the North and South Brother Islands, at the entrance to the Durian Strait, faded with the dawn. Off to the north-east, mercifully hidden by the bulk of Abang Besar, was the O.P. on Galang Baru. It was going to take them most of the day to clear the Temiang Strait into the relative safety of the open sea. Ted Carse, in the good plain English of his log entries, gives a vivid account of the hopes and hazards of the next fourteen days:

"*September 18, 10.30:* Steaming east-south-east and approaching the southern entrance of Temiang Strait. Sing yo! ho! for Borneo. All the crew are feeling the strain of long hours and ceaseless watching. Unless we get a quiet time soon I will have to issue benzedrine. I have the same feeling but have now only had four hours off the wheel in about thirty-six and look like being here until we clear the Strait at least.

"The barometer to-day stands at 29.86, the highest for some days. The sky is overcast and the wind fresh. As we are still in the Strait there is no sea to speak of. Well, it's us for the great open spaces. It's marvellous how one's ideas can change in the space of a few days. Two days ago I thought this was a dangerous run, but after the last two days it's like an evening at home. My right eye is very sore and is giving me quite a lot of trouble. I hope we get a chance to anchor at Tanjong Puting.

"*September 19:* Yesterday passed off quietly. Everyone on board has had eight hours' sleep and all feel refreshed and well.

"Our present job reminds me very much of the anxious father waiting outside the maternity ward for news. The only difference is that his worry and anxiety pass, as a rule, with the arrival of the triplets in a few hours or so, while ours is to drag on for a fortnight and when the time does come we expect a lusty overgrown family of six. Steering due east about a hundred miles from Temiang so as to cross most of the shipping routes at right angles. Sighted a junk about six miles to starboard at 1000 and at 1600 sighted the Esprit group of islands on the port bow. When abeam we will change course southwards towards Greig Shoals. This should keep us well out of shipping routes.

"*September 20:* Our bottom is getting very dirty, long green weeds about four inches long all round, so we will have to run to Borneo and put in a day or so scraping. As we don't pick up the party till the 1st we have plenty of time. I hope they are finding it as easy as we are and that they had a successful trip.

"*September 21:* Still good weather, still no sightings. Large shoals of porpoises which were playing all round us yesterday again joined company with us.

"*0800:* Our cook is certainly living up to his name of Pancake Andy. We get them at least once a day. When the cruise commenced pancakes were one of my favourites; at the present rate if I ever look at one again I shall be sick. I must admit however that they are far more appetising than hard biscuits. What wouldn't we give for a loaf of bread and a good sirloin of steak. When the cook was engaged for the trip he was in the Sappers. His cooking qualifications were that he was a fair motor mechanic and had a rough idea of how to cook pancakes. He has on the whole done an excellent job.

"Acting Leading Seaman Cain is also another excellent hand. Capable in all branches of seamanship, willing to work at any time and for any length of time and always cheerful. He is having a little trouble with his eyes also. The Japanese news broadcasts are now our main delight. We listen to hear if there is any news of our party, of which no news is good news."

During the day they sighted the Leman group and passed between Buan and Pelapsis islands. No ships were seen for forty-eight hours, although during the night of the twenty-second they found themselves in the middle of a violent electric storm. Over an arc of ninety degrees, the lightning played continuously for an hour and a half, at times looking like neon signs, with the light threads extending in all directions, and at others illuminating the whole arc like flood lighting. There was never more than a second or two without one flash or more.

The whole of the following week they cruised up and down among the scattered islands off the southwest coast of Borneo on either side of the Tanjong Sambar cape. Although they sighted a number of fishing craft and junks engaged in coastal trade, slight alterations of course always succeeded in carrying them clear, and they were never challenged or closed. There were so few of them left aboard *Krait* that watch-keeping duties had to be doubled up and the strain started to tell. Young alternated between his wireless set and keeping look-out, and Crilly had to take time off from his cooking to understudy Morris as quartermaster. Even off watch, they were only able to catnap at best, as they were never able to relax their vigilance. The admirable Crilly did his best to relieve the strain:

"Our cook is experimenting," Carse wrote in his log on the twenty-third. "To-day he made what was quite a good resemblance of a steamed pudding. So close a resemblance in fact the crew have specially requested that instead of a sample like to-day he puts on a meal of it tomorrow. I feel a little lost to-day as we have had no pancakes so far and I still prefer them to biscuits.

"So far since we left the party I have been able to run by dead reckoning and by careful treatment my eyes are becoming better. I hope they are all right for our final flutter homeward. I intend to anchor to-night and get busy on the bottom tomorrow.

"*September 24:* The sea is too choppy at present to think of scraping her, but I am hoping for a decrease in wind velocity this afternoon. This waiting about is the worst part of the trip so far. If one had an objective it would not be so bad, or if the weather was fine and we could work on the ship. We have lately been rising to the seas, but to-day the waves are so close together and so steep that they just curl over and topple on to the fo'castle, while the wind picks up the spindrift and whirls it away. Well, the show is on tonight and that completes half our estimated time in Japanese waters. After that it remains only to pick them up and return home. Let's hope that after all this worry they will be successful and have some good reports as well about the defences of Singapore. If the trip is a success we are thinking of re-naming the *Krait. The Singapore Terror* seems more appropriate.

"The wind and sea have continued to rise and are both now about 6, scattered clouds still hang about but the rain squalls have gone. Apart from the weather, which has made everything on board wet and clammy, this has so far been another uneventful day.

"*September 25:* Well, we are waiting for the first Japanese broadcast now to tell us the news of Singapore. Let's hope it has the honourable Jap running round in circles for a few days. The state of the sea is still too rough to do any scraping but the wind should drop this afternoon.

"We are again rounding Tanjong Sambar, as we will get a little protection from this trade wind and should be able to do our scraping. This afternoon's session gave no indication of any raid on Singapore, so we will try again tonight. This waiting for something to happen is not easy and news of the raid would be very welcome. Not only would it assure us of the welfare of the party but would indicate that our main object has been achieved.

"The trip, according to schedule, has now entered its second half, and everyone on board is pining for land. It is now twenty-three days since we have set foot on shore and the space at our disposal is very limited for exercise, so we feel it more than on a big ship. Again, half the time, it is as much as one can do to stand up without hanging on, let alone do any exercise. If everything runs to schedule from now on we should clear Lombok Strait on the night of October 9. With extra good fortune we may possibly make it by the 8th. This means Exmouth by the 14th or 15th, or about twenty days. We'll sure make the welkin ring that day.

"*September 26, 0415:* We ran into a heavy rain storm and managed to collect about forty or fifty gallons of water to replenish our tanks and got a wash in fresh water for a change.

"*0600:* At daybreak two sailing ships were anchored within about two miles of us and as we were then on a south-south-east course going into the wind, we held on. At about 0630 they hoisted sail and one proceeded northwards quickly dropping astern. The other started beating into the wind and looked like coming too close to us so we altered course to north-north-west.

"*0830:* Sailing ship still within a few miles on our port beam but as we seemed to be gradually drawing ahead we altered course to south and held on.

"*Midday:* So far no news has come over the wireless about Singapore. All they seem to be doing is to try and impress the civilian population of the vast superiority of the Imperial Japanese Air Force and the vast amount of men that will be needed to take their gains off them.

"*1300:* In sight of Bawal Island ten miles distant. No sails in sight so stopped engines and commenced scraping bottom. The weed is so long and covers all the bottom below the waterline that it will be a very long and arduous job to do it at all well. Our only real hope would be to run her aground somewhere on a high tide and scrape her at low water and as at present I am trying to keep out of sight of prying eyes until we have picked up the party, I don't want to do that. It is probably taking a little off our speed but as that at best is under 7 knots, that is not really important. All hands are at present doing their best and I will now give them a hand.

"*1600:* Still drifting, one sail in sight beating to windward and close in shore. Scraping still proceeding. A light breeze is springing up from south-east. If the weather remains fine we will anchor here tonight in 14 fathoms. If there is any sea at all running, this ship is the most contrary of all. She insists on lying at right angles to her cable and the sea. And can she roll. Everything that is movable goes from one side of the deck to the other. To-day we are also splicing a hemp hawser to our anchors so that we can anchor and weigh in comparative silence. Still no news from Singapore. We will shortly have to make tracks for the rendez-vous and I would feel a lot easier in mind if some news of the event was announced.

"As the only clothes worn nowadays are *sarongs* we will probably be forgetting when we get back to civilisation and all be arrested for indecent exposure. I think that this habit has been the main reason for us not having contracted any skin diseases or other ailments, which are usually common after being cooped up and having only tinned foods to eat.

"There is one thing I am heartily sick of and that is hanging round the coast of Borneo trying to dodge all comers. It seems peculiar that we should be drifting round the China Sea with men working in a dinghy alongside, scraping the bottom, on a beautiful day, just as if Mr. Tojo had not been heard of. Well, it is now 1900, so we will anchor, set watches and bed down for the night. We have scraped all the weed we could off the bottom, got all our hawsers ready and are ready now for the next step.

"*September 27, 0600:* Wind and sea very light from north-east. I hope this does not mean the change of the monsoon, as I want to get through Lombok before that happens. At daybreak three sailing ships were in sight inshore from us. They were apparently lying at anchor, as shortly after they were observed hoisting sail. All seemed to be going in a southerly direction towards Tanjong Sambar, so when we weighed we proceeded into the wind on a northerly course towards Tanjong Beras. This coast seems to be a favourite night anchorage for these sailing craft. I don't know if this means that they are prohibited from sailing at night or whether it is just them taking natural precautions. Two of these ships were three-masted junks and as a rule they just set a course for somewhere and go there non-stop.

"Yesterday Leading Telegraphist Young picked up what appeared to be a recall signal to a flight of nine 'planes, each of which replied independently and then closed down. They seemed close to him but we did not see them. I think this means that we would be safer if we keep under way during daylight hours anyway. It might also mean that they have caught the party or abandoned the search. We should know which on the

1st when we make the rendez-vous. So far no news at all and we are all keyed up to know how things are going.

"The sea is like a looking glass, not a ripple anywhere. Still no news from or of Singapore.

"*September 28:* Well that's another day over, we just have to loiter to-day and then go hell for leather for our party. At daybreak we were in sight of Black Rock and shortly afterwards Vogelnest Islands came into view on the starboard bow.

"*0830:* We have all just had a beautiful cold shower. At 0800 we ran into a very heavy rain shower. It was appreciated by all. The crew are now busily engaged in filling our water tanks. The rain shows no sign of diminishing. It is lovely to feel clean even if it is only for a few hours, as tomorrow we will have to blacken up again for our run across to the Lingga Islands and up Temiang Strait. We are still without any news of our party and have no signs of any pursuit or hullabaloo.

"*1300:* Our black dye is running low. We have only enough to paint twice more and I think the most important times will be when we approach and pass through the Straits of Temiang and Lombok. For this reason we have to keep far enough away to prevent people on passing ships remarking on our whiteness. This would probably cause *kampong* gossip which might eventually reach the ears of the Japanese.

"*September 28:* We have spent the day dodging sailing craft and jockeying for a suitable position for our dash across the China Sea tomorrow afternoon. We are all filled with anxiety as we have had no news at all of the party and this does not seem too good to us."

Their long wait was over. Anything was preferable to the aimless hanging around to which they had been subjected for the previous ten days. They had all become a little edgy with the constant strain and inclined to snap at each other when the slightest thing went wrong. They all had perfect confidence in Carse's seamanship, and had not the slightest doubt that, providing they were not intercepted, he would get *Krait* back to the rendez-vous, but he did not have the fire and special magic of Lyon, Davidson, or Page, and the crew had become a little restive under him.

For his part, he found them distinctly difficult to control. "In future operations it would be better if the crew were older than, say, 25," he wrote in his log. "The younger members do not seem to realise their responsibilities as they should and have to be told continuously to do their ordinary routine duties. Unless told daily, their arms are never cleaned and on watch they tend to become slack. A cruise like this does not seem to provide them with the excitement they crave. A fight with a patrol boat would not find them wanting but might prove fatal to the result of the cruise. I hope that now I have fully awakened them to their responsibilities. If I have not succeeded in so doing, the fault is their own stupidity and carelessness."

The twenty-ninth dawned dull and overcast, with

poor visibility, ideal conditions for their return dash. The cantankerousness and difficulties of the previous days seemed to disappear as Crilly brought round the pancakes and tea. Even the somewhat gloomy Carse sensed the change as he wrote:

"*1000:* Well, we feel a little more cheerful now, although we have had no news of the party, as we now have a definite rendez-vous and are going to it. Anxiety remains however, as we do not know if we are walking into a trap or not. The Leman islands are now on the starboard bow. We pass them to the southward.

"At 1500 we had 292 miles to cover to get to the entrance to Temiang and 47 hours to do it in. This should give even us a slight margin. From there we have a run of 25 miles to the rendez-vous, which we want to make at dusk about 1900 and five hours in which to do that distance, so we should have no difficulty in doing that.

"The clouds and rain will keep dangers away to-day, so that leaves only tomorrow and the next day to worry about. Tomorrow should be safe enough, but the following day, when we have to take Temiang in the daylight, should be our first indication of how the search is going on. Then if we can gather up our party and do the return through Temiang by midnight of the 1st, we should be safe until we approach Lombok, as this coast of Borneo knows the *Krait* by sight now.

"*1800:* Wind backed to south-south-west and increased in velocity to Force 7, causing a very short choppy sea of Force 4-5 with white horses everywhere. At times, beating into the sea, we were making practically no way at all. We just seemed to be pivoting about the wheel house. First the bows would rise and as they commenced to fall the stern commenced to rise. By 2100 the wind dropped suddenly and shortly after it the sea dropped also.

"*September 30:* And another day gone. Tomorrow night we should know our fate, for if we make contact safely the job is almost done.

"*0600:* Wind and sea from west Force 1. Scattered clouds mainly round the horizon, visibility good. No news of the party last night so we will have to try again this afternoon. Once again we appear as natives. The thinner for the dye is running low and this time we are really black. During the day we had several squalls at times, the wind approaching 4. We also had a fresh water shower.

"*October 1, 0730:* Sighted Lingga Island. At times heavy squalls blot out everything, at others the visibility is quite good. On the whole this is an ideal day for our run up Temiang Strait.

"*1700:* The wind has now dropped again and the sea is without a ripple. Verily a day of changes. The clouds have now passed away and much to my disgust the visibility is excellent. We are passing Kentar light with about five miles' clearance. There are no suspicious signs and no movement. We still have forty miles to go to meet the party, so will not get there until nearly midnight.

"*1720:* Steamship's smoke visible astern. By her

smoke she is travelling east-south-east, bound apparently from Singkep. No masts or superstructure to be seen.

"*1735:* Ship has two masts, one funnel. Course now appears to be east. Shortly after crossing our wake, she altered course north by east towards the Rhio Strait. At dark we could distinguish her funnel, bridge and masts, but no hull. By dark we were still about five miles from the Strait."

It took them another six hours to fight the tide in the narrows and it was nearly midnight before Carse turned *Krait* to the south and edged towards Pompong Island. The engine was throttled right down and Carse relied on the tide to carry them into the bay where they had unstepped *Krait's* mast and made ready for the attack fifteen days earlier.

The island was little more than a greater area of darkness in the pervading black of the night. There was no moon, and most of the brilliant tropical stars were obscured by scurrying cloud banks. Mercifully the sea was calm. Everyone except Carse in the wheelhouse and McDowell in the engine room was on deck, peering desperately into the gloom for some sign of movement. It seemed impossible that people who had been 400 miles apart could meet again on this one tiny speck in the centre of Japanese-occupied Asia. They were so keyed up that hardly a word was exchanged. This was no time for false alarms.

Crilly, ever mindful of his companions' appetites, slipped back to his cubby hole of a galley to trim the oil burners right down. Boarded in on all four sides, there was little likelihood of their faint glow being visible, and he wanted to make sure that if the attack party did come aboard, there would be hot *kai* and the inevitable stew ready for them. He had cooked up a particularly good brew that evening, with more onions and meat than usual.

At a whispered order from Carse, Cain and Marsh let down the small anchor. The hemp hawser ran out with a barely audible splash, but the tide was so strong that *Krait* threatened to drag, so the small anchor had to be hurriedly hoisted in and the large one dropped instead. They were now less than a hundred yards from the shore. Suddenly Berryman, who had the sharpest eyes of them all, thought he saw a movement on the beach where a tiny strip of sand separated jungle from sea.

He grabbed Morris' arm next to him and pointed. Sure enough there were people there and it looked as if they were launching a boat. This was no time to take chances. It might be inquisitive Malayan fishermen. At worst one of the party might have been captured alive and tortured into giving away the rendez-vous. Grabbing their guns, they stood ready to repel boarders. If it was a boat there was only one of them, and about the size of a folboat at that. Now they could pick up the slight phosphorescence as the paddles dipped into the water. The canoe was heading straight for them. Just as the tension became too much to bear, a hoarse hail came out of the night: "Ahoy

Krait." It was unmistakeably Davidson's voice, and with him safe and sound was Poppa Falls. In a moment the canoe was alongside and the two men were being helped aboard by willing hands.

5

THE FACE AT THE PORTHOLE

FOR THE SIX MEN OF THE ATTACK TEAMS, THE PARTING from *Krait* had been an even greater wrench. Although the vital stage of the expedition lay ahead of them, they felt very lonely, deposited a thousand miles inside the enemy lines, faced by a fortnight abandoned to their own slender resources. Lyon was very worried as he stood on the sandy beach and watched *Krait's* familiar, ridiculous outline fade into the night—worried about Carse's eyes being able to stand up to the strain of the pin-point navigation which must bring them back to Pompong at the end of the month, worried about *Krait's* ability to give an account of herself now that her firepower had been reduced by half, worried that the only other two men with real knowledge of local lore and jungle survival, Davidson and Page, were standing beside him and that there was no one left aboard to hold the youngsters together should anything go wrong.

His other five companions gave him no qualms. They were fighting fit in spite of the fatigues of the voyage and the unbearable strain of the last forty-eight hours.

Davidson, with his inexhaustible energy and inventiveness, tough as oak; Page, intelligent, resourceful, and utterly reliable; Falls, the young Greek god, powerful, tireless, ever alert; Jones, with his power-packed, thickset body and ready smile; and Huston, the "Baby" of the party, dogged, endlessly willing and making up in will power and determination for his lack of years. If they could not get to Singapore and back, then no one could.

For the moment they felt safe enough. In his quick reconnaissance from the dinghy into the jungle earlier in the night, Davidson had found nothing to indicate that this part of Panjang was in any way frequented. The folboats and the stores had been dragged up into the undergrowth and all was quiet, the breathless hush which even in the tropics precedes the dawn. Around and above them the huge ficus trees were whispering in the light airs. Beyond the horse-shoe of rocks that hemmed in their little haven, the treetops were etched in sharp profile against the glittering slate grey of the night sky, with the clouds slowly building up for the morning overcast.

It was an idyllic, peaceful scene. After the sour smell of diesel oil, hot tar, and timbers and the lingering fish stench from *Krait*'s ancient bilges, the jungle scents were almost overpowering in their sweetness. Ground lilies and a flowering tree with white midnight blossoms made the air round them almost tangible. They breathed it deeply, gathering strength for the trial that lay ahead.

There was nothing further they could do that night.

Their muscles ached from the unloading and their brains were tired. Ducking back into the bush a few yards under cover, each of them burrowed out a hip hole under his groundsheet, wrapped himself in a blanket, and to the soothing rustle of the jungle insects was on the instant asleep.

The respite only lasted three hours, but was infinitely refreshing. As they sat round their first breakfast of emergency rations they held a council of war. The drop had been carried out ahead of schedule and they could afford to take the next two days resting, getting their land legs—each of them still swayed on solid ground with the inbuilt movement of *Krait*—building up their dump, and sorting out their stores. Davidson, the best silent tracker, moved off into the jungle to see how safe their hide-out was. Huston, sent down with a rake to remove all traces of their landing, was soon back with the encouraging report that the tide had obliterated everything up to the high-water mark and that a legion of bustling little land crabs had made his work quite unnecessary.

Davidson was equally reassuring. There was a native fishing village about a quarter of a mile away on the other side of the spit of land, but no sign of any tracks leading in their direction. There was no apparent reason beyond rank carelessness why they should be discovered. They were so well trained that they could move about and work for hours without making a sound audible beyond twenty yards. Their rope-soled jungle boots were noiseless and these could always be discarded in favour of thick socks if they were willing to risk lacerating feet a little softened since the Refuge Bay days by the long sea voyage.

They started to redistribute and cache their stores. About twenty-five yards back in the jungle they found a fresh water hole, part of a series of rocky pools, which made an ideal dump. An overhanging rock shielded a generous space guarded by growing ferns. Gradually they stacked the carboys of distilled water brought for an emergency, the tins of rations, the grenades and ammunition, batteries and spare equipment, which were to replenish their return journey. With one of their number always standing guard behind a tree giving a clear view of the beach, they worked calmly, quietly, purposefully, and wordlessly until everything was sorted out.

There was time to spare. When a family of otters emerged from the undergrowth along the water course, they all paused to watch. This was a good sign. Their gambolling could only mean that the animals regarded this corner of the jungle as safe. The beach was christened Otter Bay in their honour.

Again they paused when the unmistakeable pop-pop of a diesel came echoing over the point, but they saw nothing. As Lyon took over from Page at the observation post, the Australian was able to report that the junks and fishing craft out at sea all seemed to be moving about their normal business. During the morning a succession of aircraft came over fairly high from the north. They seemed to form part of some regular patrol, returning in due course from the south, and after a while the party ceased to be disturbed by them.

The forty-eight hours that followed were the best of the whole trip. They lazed around, wallowed in the fresh water, scrubbing off the filth of the voyage and enjoying the unspeakable luxury of cleaning their teeth in something other than pure brine. There was the occasional scare. For a tense half hour the shrilling of birds up the hill made them think that some native was after all making his way over from the village, but the noises in the undergrowth resolved themselves into a troop of monkeys, who surveyed the party with chirpy curiosity and then gradually leap-frogged away again. During the evening, they heard the disturbing plop-plop of the same diesel. Clearly there was a patrol boat making an irregular inspection of the area. They heard it again on the second night, but at a different time, and it was obviously an inquisitive adversary of whom they would have to beware.

The evening of September 20 found them in magnificent trim. The stores and equipment for the three folboats were checked and rechecked—food and water for at least eight days, charts and the Admiralty register of enemy shipping, arms greased and ammunition inspected for mildew, and, above all, the precious limpet mines themselves. Here Page was the expert. The rods down which they were slid to be clipped on the side of ships with their magnets were cleaned and oiled until they ran like silk. The detonators, the hinges for the magnets, every working part was inspected.

They represented the last stage in the long haul across from Sydney and nothing could be allowed to impede their successful functioning. Three sets of them went into each canoe, together with the magnetic hold-fast which enabled them to hold steady in the tide as the canoe came alongside its target and each successive mine was fixed. Everything was in order and they were replaced inside their watertight containers. Then came the boats themselves. Every bamboo strut, every inch of the rubberised canvas, was run over by keen eyes and probing fingers for the slightest snag or flaw. The waist bands which fastened round the operators and prevented a single drop of water reaching the inside of the boat were checked for the slightest puncture; so were their hoods and protective clothing. Everything had survived the pitching and tossing of *Krait's* hot hold without a mark. They were ready to go.

Fully loaded, with its two operatives, the seaman in front and the officer to correct the course and speed behind, each canoe weighed some 800 pounds. They were low and sluggish in the water, but to ensure success they could not carry less. Once the mines and half the rations had gone, it would be a very different matter and even tired paddlers should be able to make them bounce back on the return journey. After a last survey of the hide, with Page giving the natural camouflage a few final touches, the canoes were launched about seven o'clock in the evening of September 20.

They stood out a little to sink their cans and debris

in deep water and had just taken up their arrowhead formation, with Davidson and Falls in the leading boat, when they again heard the menacing plop-plop of the patrol boat's diesel. They inched in under the blackness of the trees again and waited. This time they could see the source of the noise.

Down from the north, about half a mile out, at slow speed, came the outline of a powerful naval launch. What it was seeking they could not tell, but as it made no attempt to stand in towards them it was obviously not looking for the canoes. Once it had passed, they took up position again and started paddling north-westwards themselves.

They stopped for five minutes every hour to drink a little water or eat a piece of chocolate and murmur a few comments on their progress. They were loping along quite comfortably against a slight tide and, so far, navigation had not presented any great problem. It was just as well, as the magnets and metal aboard completely disrupted their compasses and they could only steer by the stars, dead reckoning, and the chart details they each had memorised.

By midnight they had covered ten miles and were at the entrance to the Bulan Strait. They decided to carry on another three miles to the diminutive island of Pulau Bulat, the furthest point *Krait* had reached during their anxious cruise on the seventeenth. It had then appeared to be an uninhabited knoll with a sandy beach, ideal for their purpose, as it would enable them to spy out the narrow passage ahead between the islands of Boelan and Batam, which led another fifteen miles or so due north-west to the Singapore Strait and their destination.

While Lyon's and Page's canoes stood off, Davidson went in to reconnoitre. It was indeed ideal. From a sandy spit they could run the folboats in under the thick, arching roots of a clump of mangroves, providing perfect cover with minimum effort.

The faint glow of the lights of Singapore had beckoned them from the northern horizon, although they were not in as good a position to see them as they had been from *Krait* further out in the channel. It was enough to make their target tangible and everyone felt a tingling in his blood as they cooked their cursory supper and lay down for their early morning sleep. There was plenty of native shipping moving up and down the Strait the next day and, although a junk and a single native *kolek* came rather too close for comfort, they felt so secure that they spent the afternoon bathing off their sandspit and Davidson even took a photograph of them. They would have been better advised to get all the sleep they could, but with their excitement mounting, the heat, and the buzz of insects, no one succeeded in taking a siesta. Their high spirits after the welcome swim were sufficient compensation.

That evening, as they passed up the Bulan Strait, their troubles started. Narrow enough already, it is so dotted with islands that at many points even the main passage is less than half a mile wide, and Davidson, as navigator, had extreme difficulty in determining their course. At times it looked as if there was no way through the shadowy lumps of hill and jungle ahead. What made the journey infinitely worse was the proliferation of fishing *pagars*, their myriad kerosene lamps threatening detection and causing the party to make wide detours. It took Lyon and Davidson half the night to decide how to deal with them.

The Malays, in narrow channels like Bulan with a good run of fish, catch them by setting out a web of nets suspended from stakes, along which the shoal is induced to run to the central netting area, where a moored hulk or houseboat, with a family in residence, awaits their coming. At night a powerful kerosene lamp is suspended over the water and helps to attract the fish like moths to a flame. Slung horizontally along the bottom from the stakes is a large square net, which, on a given signal, is rapidly hauled up with a generous catch of fish weighing down its centre.

The lamps are usually fixed a few feet above the water. Providing they are hung from a boat, it is not too difficult a matter to gauge the distance away from the reflection, but if they are mounted on a fixed stake, as is not infrequently the case, the calculation can be wildly out, depending on the state of the tide.

The canoe crews found that the more powerful lights were visible anything up to eight miles away, but their judgment of distance was often hopelessly at fault. One such light that they estimated as being at least three miles distant was in fact only a quarter of a mile away and they were almost on it before they sheered off. Another that looked as if it was only a couple of hundred yards away proved to be a couple of miles off. They were chiefly worried about the submerged stakes puncturing the bottom of their fragile canoes, although they were making such slow progress against the tide that the risk of real damage was not serious.

After one scare, when they were within fifty yards of a *pagar*, near enough to hear the inhabitants talking, they realised that the light was in its way a form of protection. The fishermen were concentrating on the water to watch the movement of the fish and were so blinded by the glare that they could see nothing outside its immediate radius. Even the splash of a paddle did not seem to disturb them in any way. They probably took it for a fish leaping. The other advantage was that the canoes could always reckon on at least a couple of fathoms of water in the vicinity of any *pagar*, as otherwise it would not have been deep enough for the fish to run.

All these alarms had slowed the canoes down most disquietingly. By the time dawn threatened they had covered barely a dozen miles and instead of being out of the Strait were only halfway up it. They had no time to reconnoitre a proper hiding place for the day and decided to make for the Batam shore near the village of Sagilang.

As they were rounding the tip of a smaller island off shore, Page's canoe was caught in a shallow tide-rip and, momentarily out of control, rammed Lyon's craft amidships with an ugly splintering noise. The two canoes lurched apart. Neither had been holed and the canvas skins were intact, but something had happened to Lyon's canoe which they never entirely succeeded in repairing. Although the strained ribs were replaced with spares, the keel seemed to have been bent out of true. It became very heavy to paddle and imposed an additional strain on Lyon and Huston to keep up with the others.

They turned into the first mangrove swamp and secured the canoes as best they might. It was a sorry contrast to their comfortable hide on Bulat. It was infested with mosquitoes and sandflies and, after an hour's uneasy sleep spreadeagled over the roots and rocks, they woke to find that they were directly opposite a village on the island of Boyan, only three hundred yards across the narrow channel. They could not smoke, they could not talk, they could not cook, and cowered among the inadequate roots as an incessant stream of small craft passed all day across their "front door." Lyon had learnt his lesson. Whatever else they did, they must always allow sufficient time at the end of the night's paddling to find and properly inspect a suitable hide. A couple more sleepless days like this and they would all be completely exhausted.

By now it was the twenty-second and they were falling behind schedule. They could hardly wait for dusk and as soon as the light had faded forced their tiring muscles to propel them north again. The night was a complete contrast to the last. The fishing *pagars* thinned out as the channel cleared and widened. The tide was either in their favour or slack, and by half past eight they had reached the north-west corner of

Batam Island. It was as if the curtain had gone up on a brightly lit stage set. The whole of Singapore Roads opened up before them. Dead ahead, not four miles distant, was the island of Pulau Sambu, which Lyon and Davidson remembered as the former Dutch oil depot, brightly illuminated as if there was a night shift working. Only five or six miles beyond lay the vast twinkling panorama of Singapore itself.

So confident had the Japanese become after a year and a half of undisturbed occupation, with their outer perimeter still two thousand miles away, the Straits leading to Singapore mined and guarded, and the whole area well out of range of any Allied bombing base available at the time, that peace-time conditions prevailed. Low in the water as they were, the canoe crews were unable to distinguish individual lights along the waterfront. All they could see was the suffused glow. Their task had been made at once easier and more difficult. They would not have the slightest problem in finding their way into the harbour, but that blaze of light, even with blacked-out and camouflaged operatives, spelt danger. As they watched, a searchlight swung across the Straits, catching the treetops of the surrounding islands in its beam.

For their final hide and attack base, Lyon had selected Pulau Dongas, a small island lying just off the north coast of Batam and due south-east of Singapore, just behind Pulau Sambu. Paddling evenly now, with the west-east tide, they reached it just after midnight. Lyon had remembered it from his pre-war sailing days as entirely uninhabited, with an all-important supply of fresh water. There was an extensive swamp on the south side and a sandy spit at its northern head which should provide an excellent landing place. So indeed it proved to be. The canoes ran past its jungle-covered hump, and Davidson, in his usual role of scout, went in ahead. He returned full of enthusiasm. The sand beach ran in under mangroves, providing perfect cover and a much more extensive and comfortable hide even than on Bulat. The canoes were hauled up, with some difficulty as the tide was low, and, with one of their number, as always, on watch, the other five collapsed into sleep.

They had touched the limit of human endurance. In the three days since leaving Panjang none of them had had more than half a dozen hours' sleep. Lyon was the worst hit. For him the physical strain was compounded by the responsibility and concentration of leadership. This was the testing time for his plan. Davidson was a superb foil, but only Lyon could supply the detailed, instinctive knowledge of the terrain, the snap decision on tactics, choicc and change of hide, and, with his knowledge of the Malay language, any hint from the overhcard conversation of fishermen and villagers that their plan needed to be modified. He had lost weight and was looking gaunt and hollow-cheeked. Reading his mood, his companions redoubled their efforts, taking the minor details off the shoulders of the one man on whom everything depended.

They could afford to spend the next day resting. A detailed search of the island revealed not a single sign of human habitation or movement. Their sole companions were a colony of large black- and yellow-striped sea iguanas and a couple of small crocodiles. While the others remained in the hide to check their canoes and equipment, Lyon and Davidson climbed to the highest point of the island to begin their watch on the Roads and work out their plan of attack. They had hoped to find some supplement to their meagre and uninspiring rations, but, as Lyon was to write later in his report:

"The canoe parties drank water whenever they found it, without boiling, with no bad results. It was, however, always taken from a scooped-out hole and not from a stagnant pool. Had there been habitations in the vicinity, it would have been boiled. The old well on Pulau Dongas was stagnant, but very careful scooping kept the water from being stirred up and no ill effects resulting from drinking it.

"The popular idea that tropical islands abound with luscious fruits is a complete misconception as regards this area. Neither fruit nor vegetable in any form was found wild—certain neglected coconuts, however, would have afforded some sustenance and could have been gathered. Vegetable gardens in the vicinity of villages could have been raided, but much reliance on this form of food should not be placed when planning operations in this territory. Wild pigs are to be found on certain of the bigger islands and bird life is plentiful; green pigeons, doves, etc. being able, with patience, to be trapped. Game of any description is not to be expected within a mile of native habitations."

Ivan Lyon as a schoolboy at Harrow. (Lent by Mrs. Ann Gordon)

Lyon as a subaltern in the Gordon Highlanders in Malaya. (Copyright *Straits Times*, Singapore)

Cabinet portrait of Lyon as a subaltern in the Gordon Highlanders. (Copyright Lenare, Hanover Square, London)

Lieutenant Colonel Ivan Lyon, D.S.O., M.B.E., on Operation "Rimau," with the tiger *(rimau)* tattooed on his chest. (Courtesy of Lieutenant Colonel W. W. Chapman)

Lyon as a young subaltern in the Gordon Highlanders in Singapore prior to the outbreak of war. (Courtesy of Mrs. Ann Gordon)

Keppel Harbour, Singapore, ablaze as British prepare to surrender. (Imperial War Museum, London)

Lyon at the tiller of the *Hin Lee*. (Courtesy of Mrs. Ann Gordon)

The *Hin Lee* off the coast of Ceylon after Lyon and his companions had been picked up by the M.V. *Anglo-Canadian.* (Courtesy of Mrs. Ann Gordon)

The *Hin Lee* sunk by gunfire from the *Anglo-Canadian*. (Courtesy of Mrs. Ann Gordon)

The M.V. *Krait*. (Australian War Memorial)

The M.V. *Krait* in the South China Seas with the crew in their camouflage paint. Lyon in foreground. (Australian War Memorial)

Lyon and his companions bathing off Bulat Island during their canoe journey to Singapore. (Australian War Memorial)

View from the island of Subar, forward base for the "Jaywick" attack on Singapore. (Australian War Memorial)

Lyon observing the results of the "Jaywick" attack from Dongas Island. (Australian War Memorial)

The six men of the canoe crews toasting their success after their return to Australia. (Australian War Memorial)

The tablet erected by his family in memory of Lyon on the wall of the Singapore Garrison Church. (Courtesy of Mrs. Ann Gordon)

Once a suitable observation point had been chosen, constant watch was kept by the six men in turn, plotting the position of the various ships at anchor and endeavouring to identify them with the help of the Admiralty Register they had brought with them. This went on for forty-eight hours.

"The Dongas observation post was opposite and eight miles distant from Kallang," Lyon noted in his report. "In conditions of good visibility it was possible to see into Keppel Harbour. A night watch was kept until 2300 hours on September 23, revealing no signs of any defensive activity. There was no black-out in Singapore and the lights of cars driving down Beach Road could be clearly seen. No harbour or navigation lights were burning and all shipping was stationary.

"The following day we were well rested and maintained a keen watch, during which we carefully scrutinised both shore and shipping. There was no change to be seen in the general outline of the city. A row of five to seven tall wireless masts have been constructed on the site of the former Paya Lebar station and there is a single mast on the roof of tho Cathay Building. On the southernmost point of St. John's Island there is now a small signal station. At Sambu, three miles from our observation post, all visible oil tanks were still as left by the Dutch. There was tremendous activity on the western side of the island. The hammering of plates and drone of engines by day and night suggested either ship repair or building.

"In the harbour and Roads of Singapore there was considerable movement of shipping. At no time was there less than 100,000 tons at the same time. Ships arrived from the east, either singly or in groups; none of these exceeded five ships and only one group was escorted. All were heavily laden and proceeded direct to their anchorage. Those ships seen to leave again for the east were, in many cases, lightly laden on in ballast. The point of departure for ships entering the Malacca Strait was obscured from Dongas. It is not, therefore, possible to judge the quantity of shipping leaving for the west. Absence of patrol vessels and freedom of movement by medium draught native craft convinced us that there were no mine fields in the harbour.

"During the late afternoon of September 24, a total of 65,000 tons was seen to be assembled in the Roads opposite Dongas. It was realised that unfavourable tides would render an attack on this shipping difficult, but the nature of the target was such that an attempt seemed imperative."

Among the native craft they had seen were several disreputable sisters to *Krait*. This was an encouraging thought, as it reduced the likelihood of any attention being paid to them on the return journey. They all wore a Japanese flag and the only difference was that they carried, painted on their bows, numbers and lettering as if licensed to trade between Singapore and other ports. It was a point they might have to watch.

That afternoon they plotted their targets, identifying and noting for the intelligence files back in Melbourne every ship they could see. The tankers they would ignore. It was the one type of vessel against which the limpet mine was least effective. Their main target was merchant ships. Three limpets laid along the side against the main holds would each blow a hole four or five feet in diameter and the ship must inevitably sink. Davidson and Falls, in the No. 2 canoe, were to take the group of ships lying in the Singapore Roads proper, to the east of Keppel Harbour. Of the other two, Page was to concentrate on the ships lying alongside the wharves on the island of Pulau Bukum, to the south-west of Singapore, and Lyon was to deal with the other group of ships lying in the examination anchorage between Bukum and the main island.

With the precious mines checked and double-checked again, they launched the canoes for the attack about eight o'clock at night. Everyone knew his role and there was no need for long farewells. Each man gripped the others' hand, they wished each other good luck and started off in company in their usual arrowhead formation. Readily accessible, each man carried a small rubber pellet filled with lethal cyanide. If any of them should be caught one bite brought instant death. If the attack failed, the Japanese would at least be denied the triumph of exhibiting their captives—and the crew of *Krait* would be safe.

They skirted warily past the glare of Sambu and, to their relief, as the night advanced, the lights of Singapore started to dim. Halfway to the target area, a searchlight was suddenly switched on from some high point, probably the top of the Cathay Building, swung slowly round, and then came to rest on the three folboats for a full half minute. They flicked their canoes bow on and sat transfixed. Then it continued its sweep and was as suddenly switched off. They expected every searchlight in the harbour to open up, but nothing happened. At moments of such heightened danger, every fear is justified, but it really seemed as if they had not been spotted.

They resumed their course, only to find that the increasing force of the tide started to take its toll. They turned the bows of the canoes further east to meet it, but they were barely making headway. They had now been paddling for more than three hours. Practised canoe operatives can continue for much longer without excessive fatigue, but it was becoming clear that they were rooted in mid-channel and time was running out on them. They were nowhere near any ships yet and, even in the most favourable conditions, they would have to allow at least an hour for the actual attack. At all costs they must be back in their hide by daybreak. By one o'clock in the morning the attempt had become hopeless. At Lyon's careful hail, the three canoes drew together and the bitter decision was taken to break off the attack and run for safety. They would have to try from a point further west two nights later.

The tide was an equal enemy on the return journey. It carried them well to the east of Dongas and when it started to slacken they decided to race for the hide individually. Davidson and Falls, Page and Jones, the two stronger couples, reached the mangrove swamp in time, but there was no sign of Lyon and Huston.

Wrestling with their lopsided canoe, they had lost contact.

The strain was beginning to tell on Lyon by now. All the planning, all the responsibility, and most of the worry had been his and the physical effort was starting to wrack his frail frame. He might have done better to change partners with Davidson, as Poppa Falls could paddle for two all day, but this was not Lyon's way. The make-up of the crews had long since been determined and it was essential to have a pair of fast paddlers for emergencies and spying out the land ahead.

Lyon and Huston were safe. They had battled on until they could hardly see from exhaustion and had mistaken their bearings. They landed on the wrong side of Dongas just as dawn was breaking and spent an unhappy, sleepless day in pouring rain, hiding in an outcrop of boulders.

At seven o'clock that evening, having recovered sufficiently to discover where they were, they paddled round the point to rejoin the main party, to be greeted with cries of relief. "Lieutenant Davidson had anticipated our arrival and organised a much needed hot meal," Lyon was to report tersely but gratefully. "He had also made plans for an immediate change to an alternative hide, whence an attack could be launched the following night of the 26th/27th, under favourable conditions. His prompt action on this occasion contributed greatly to the success of the expedition."

The new base, which both Lyon and Davidson had

noted from their observation post on the previous day, was the island of Subar, lying due west from them on the other side of the Bulan Strait. As soon as Lyon and Huston had rested a little they set off, with Davidson and Falls in the slow folboat, and managed to beat the tide, which ran less strongly along the northern coast of Batam, quite comfortably. Subar had no beach and no water but was mercifully uninhabited. Dawn caught them still manhandling stores and canoes over the boulders, but they managed to hide everything under bushes and behind rocks and this time slept the whole morning.

By the afternoon they were sufficiently recovered to climb up for another look at their target. There had been little change in the moored ships and they had a much better view, straight into the examination anchorage, than had been possible from Dongas. The target areas were not changed, but the plan was altered to permit Davidson and Falls to take off separately, due north, to Keppel Harbour, while the other two canoes headed in a more north-westerly direction for Pulau Bukum. That evening, the twenty-sixth, found them faced by the sixth night of eight hours' paddling out of the last seven. They were still in relatively good shape, although their legs were suffering from a curiously rubbery feeling that came from long hours spent in an unnatural position in a canoe. But they had the spur of the actual attack to keep them going.

This time the final farewells were real. They were now two days behind schedule. Some check would have to be made on the results of the attack and, although Davidson was the expedition's photographer, he and Falls, as the strongest pair, in their original boat, were to ride the easterly set of the tide on their return journey and make their way down the Rhio Strait to the east of Batam Island, doubling back thence to Panjang and then making a bee-line for Pompong to hold *Krait*. The others should be able to make Dongas again from the examination anchorage and after confirming the effects of the raid, would rejoin the rendez-vous down the Bulan Strait, the way they had come.

"Cheerio, Ivan, best of luck," said Donald Davidson, looking a little worriedly at Lyon's hollow-cheeked face, with the sleepless shadows under his eyes and the short stubble of his beard.

"The same to you, Donald. And thank you for everything. See you back at Pompong."

The others were more light-hearted, but their handgrips were not less fervent. They manhandled their slate-grey canoes over the rocks, checked the fastenings on their skin-tight black vests and hoods, climbed in to the narrow circular opening which sealed the inside of their folboats from the sea, and with a last salute of their paddles set off.

The more northerly course made possible by the change of base had made things very much easier. Davidson and Falls were across the Straits in a couple of hours, and although they kept a wary eye on a searchlight which opened up on Blakang Mati Island off to port, encountered no serious difficulties. The two men had developed a warm understanding and chatted easily, with Davidson pointing out the main buildings and sights of Singapore to his fascinated companion. It hardly seemed possible that they could be passing unobserved right across the inner harbour of this Japanese bastion. As they grew closer in, they muffled their voices until Davidson pointed out the unmistakeable triad pylons of the Keppel Harbour boom ahead of them.

Just as they altered course slightly, Falls spotted a set of navigation lights moving out at them from the night. They proved to be on a large steam tug turning into the same channel. It headed straight for them until it seemed impossible that they should not be either sighted or run down. Then, at the last moment, it turned towards Blakang Mati and they were left safe but badly shaken.

As soon as they had regained their composure they forged ahead again and to their surprise found the Tanjong Pagar end of the boom opened. The temptation was too strong for Davidson. Two days earlier, from Dongas, two large freighters had been sighted tied up alongside the wharves. If these could be sunk, they would block the entire dock for months. Unhesitatingly, Davidson turned hard aport right into Keppel Harbour. It was a mad gamble to take, as the harbour was little more than five hundred yards wide, but the tug had not succeeded in spotting them from a mere fifty yards away and Davidson was so confident of the efficacy of their camouflage that he ploughed straight in. They paddled the whole length of the wharves, but their targets had gone. The vessels in the Empire Docks behind were too brightly illuminated and too small to justify the risk involved.

As they turned and made their way out again they found two small freighters against the east wharf, but considered that they were not worthy of their attention, compared with the large ships lying out in the Roads which were their original targets. Apart from the busy unloading going on in the Empire Docks under the arc lights, there was little sign of movement in the main harbour. Davidson could scarcely credit that the Japanese had become so lax in their security, but then, as he considered ruefully, perhaps they had very little to worry about—apart from enemy folboats loaded with limpet mines. But they had obviously not thought of that.

Out through the boom again they continued due east towards the shipping in the Roads. Here it was merely a question of taking their choice. The look-outs must have been unbelievably slack, as the operation went like clockwork. They might just as well have been attacking abandoned hulks in Sydney Harbour. Swinging at their anchors, the bows of all the ships were pointed towards Singapore in the current and, as the canoe drifted down the port side of each, they were nicely in the shadow from the lights of Singapore. The tide was running at about half a knot, perfect for their purpose.

Firm-fingered, they went through the drill. Out with the hold-fast and, as Davidson steadied the canoe, Falls set the fuse, slipped a mine down on its placing stick, and snapped the magnets against the hull well under water. It was as easy as that. Release the hold-fast, drift down the length of cordtex to the side of the next hold, and plant another mine. Three times and that was the ration. Slowly and silently they drifted down to the next victim, which they had identified as the *Taisyo Maru*, which they had seen from Dongas. Ignoring a 10,000-ton tanker, they carefully chose three substantial cargo vessels of at least 6000 tons' displacement. The third one had arc lights burning on deck, illuminating the surrounding water, but so confident were they now that nothing could deter them. As they worked, they could hear the chiming clock on Singapore's Victoria Hall counting out the quarter hours.

By half past one it was all over. The placing stick and hold-fast were dropped silently over the side. The mines were timed to blow at five o'clock. They had less than three hours in which to cross the Straits again and find a hide on the north shore of Batam Island. Confident, triumphant, swinging easily on their paddles, they set off to the south-east.

Eight miles to the west of them, the two other canoes had remained in company to within a mile of Pulau Bukum. The time was nine o'clock, just as Davidson and Falls were slipping into Keppel Harbour. Page and Jones continued straight on to the Pulau Bukum wharves, and Lyon and Huston turned a little north to the examination anchorage. They had both had an even easier passage than the third canoe, apart from the sweep of the searchlight on Blakang Mati which had bothered Davidson and Falls.

Page and Jones found that the wharves were brightly lit, with sentries on guard at the ships' gangways. They paddled the whole length of the docks, keeping fairly well out to sea, but only saw one suitable target, an old freighter of the *Tone Maru* class. A large tanker was too heavily laden to make any attack worth while, and the third vessel, a small freighter, had a barge alongside on which a number of dockers appeared to be working under arc lights against a background of what looked like cauldrons of steam. They both watched curiously this odd spectacle for some time but could not make up their minds what the men were doing.

They drifted down to the *Tone Maru*-class freighter and slipped down their first three limpets. They could hear the Japanese crew and workmen chatting away, completely unaware of the destruction which was in store for them. Number 3 canoe then made off again to the north towards the examination anchorage. Their second target was reasonably easy to identify, with its three sets of goal-post masts. They had marked it from the Admiralty list on Subar as the *Nasusan Maru*. This whole group of ships was blacked out and, as the lights of Singapore round the corner of the mainland to the east were greatly dimmed, they had some difficulty in finding their third target, an older 6000-ton freighter. However, the tide carried them right down to it and they bumped the bow quite heavily as its dark mass emerged from the night. There can have been no look-outs on duty at all, as they heard no movement, fixed their mines without the least interruption, and immediately set off, in their turn, south-east, to the original Dongas hide.

Lyon and Huston had the most alarming experience. They were due to attack the more northerly group of ships, lying right up against Singapore Island itself. On the way they passed the *Nasusan Maru* with its three goal-post masts, but recognising that this "belonged to Page," carried on to the north.

The lights of Singapore were now hidden behind a spit of land and the two men found it completely impossible to distinguish the outlines of their targets against the background of hills. They paddled to and fro, losing a lot of time, until finally, in desperation, Lyon decided to return to the examination anchorage proper. All the ships there were blacked out, but two large tankers they had noted earlier were showing their obligatory red riding light, and rather than waste further time, he decided to attack one of these.

They had fixed one limpet on the propeller shaft and were just lowering a second, beside the engine room, when Lyon saw Huston looking upwards. He glanced up himself, and there, not ten feet above their heads, a man was watching them intently out of a porthole.

He made no sign or sound and, with an inspired reflex action, Lyon gestured impatiently to his partner to get on with the work.

There is no rational explanation for the man's complete inactivity. Whether he thought they were starving Malays picking off barnacles for the family pot there is no way of telling. He continued to watch them earnestly as they fixed the last limpet and then, with Lyon willing Huston to remain calm, withdrew his head and lighted the lamp in his cabin as they pushed off. If he lived to tell the tale, he must have been a very surprised man three hours later. "He'll soon be dead," Lyon whispered to his partner with relish.

Nevertheless, he had upset their plans and they could not risk dallying in the anchorage any longer. For all they knew the alarm would be raised at any moment. Grim with anxiety at the thought that the whole purpose of the expedition was about to be wrecked by a general alarm, they bent their backs to their paddles and fairly skimmed the swell in a straight line for Dongas.

Both western canoes reached the island safely within a few minutes of each other shortly before five o'clock. Hauling up their folboats into the mangrove hide, Page had just given Lyon an excited account of their successful attack and Lyon was just telling the other two of the extraordinary incident with the tanker when the first booming explosion was heard. It came from over on the Keppel Harbour side and was their first indication that Davidson too had been successful. Listening intently, they counted two, three, from the Keppel Harbour direction and another four from their own area. So Davidson had successfully laid all his limpets, and unless he had had as unpleasant an experience as Lyon, must be on his way to safety.

The thunder of the explosions reverberated round

the Straits and echoed back from the surrounding hills. No flashes were to be seen as the charges were all well under water. This was fantastic. They danced up and down, slapping each other on the back, whispering hoarsely and incoherently with delight, their rigid discipline not letting them down even in this moment of triumph.

The eastern sky was beginning to lighten. Within minutes of the last explosion every ship's siren in the Roads started to howl and a quarter of an hour later Singapore and Sambu Island were suddenly blacked out.

Leaving Page and Jones to see to the safety of the boats, Lyon and Huston fought their way up through the trees in the direction of the observation post. By the time they had panted and clawed their way up the hill there was just enough light for them to find their vantage point.

As dawn came up, they could see that most of the ships in the anchorage had got under way and were starting to cruise aimlessly up and down. This made it very difficult to determine what had been sunk and what had not. One ship was definitely half submerged, with her bows sticking up out of the water, over in the examination anchorage, and the big tanker, the *Sinkoku Maru,* which had given Lyon and Huston such a fright, was burning fiercely and belching out thick black smoke which covered the whole area. This left five to be accounted for and, for the time being, they had to be entered as "certainly damaged, probably sunk."

The sirens and commotion continued most of the morning. At a quarter past six a flight of twin-engined aircraft took off from Kallang airfield and roared westwards towards the Malacca Strait. They returned about two hours later and, after putting down again briefly at Kallang, took off individually and started to scour the southern approaches. One of them passed right over the Dongas hide and could be clearly identified as a twin-engined medium bomber.

By this time Page had joined the other two, leaving Jones to watch, bringing a welcome sackful of rations. They were too excited and intent on the activity in the Roads to eat very much, but nibbled absent-mindedly and thankfully at a few bars of chocolate.

At half past two another flight of nine medium bombers took off from Kallang and headed north. These they did not see return. The harbour area was patrolled throughout the day by Zero fighters and miscellaneous light aircraft, but the whole weight of the search was clearly concentrated to the north-west, the Japanese having assumed, quite reasonably, that the attack must have been launched down the Malacca Straits. Apart from the few perfunctory patrols to the south in the forenoon, no special flights were made in that direction again, an excellent omen for the party's escape.

A mass of small motor *sampans* and other various craft started to congregate in the two roadsteads where the ships had been sunk, but it was very difficult to determine through the glasses whether they were engaged in salvage work or not. No ban seemed to have been placed on the movement of shipping. Native craft continued to move across the Straits all day, while the flights of civil aircraft in and out of Kallang appeared to follow the normal pattern of the previous four days of observation.

Innumerable patrol craft and launches criss-crossed the harbour throughout the day without any apparent purpose becoming discernible in their movements. Ships continued to arrive from the north-west and appeared to pass into the inner Keppel Harbour and, as the day advanced, most of those which had been out in the Roads either joined them or steamed off towards the north.

The Japanese were completely baffled and infuriated to the point of frenzy, as much by the loss of "face" as by their shipping sunk. They turned savagely on the Allied prisoners in their hands in their search for suspects and scapegoats. One British civilian under sentence for supposed espionage activities was interrogated, beaten, starved, and tortured when he failed to admit authorship of the sabotage raid. The internees in Changi gaol suffered a murderous period. Malays and Chinese were arrested in their hundreds on suspicion of possible complicity. For months, Singapore was subjected to a wave of terror which included the infamous "Double Tenth" massacre on October 10. For this the perpetrators paid with their heads when the Allied war crimes tribunals reckoned with them after Japan had surrendered.

The high command in Singapore never did learn how the attack had been organised or from whence it came. The confidential report which was dispatched in due course to Tokyo, and extracted from the files after the war was over by the Allies, read in part: "Singapore shipping espionage has been carried out by natives under European instructions. . . . An enemy espionage affair developed early in the morning of 27th September 1943 at Singapore. It was commanded by Europeans hiding in the neighbourhood of Palai in Johore. It was carried out by Malayan criminals through a Malayan village chief and the party was composed of ten or more persons, all of them Malayans. As a result of the raid, seven ships were sunk by bombs due to a clever plan."

Although it took weeks for the information to filter through, confirmation of the success of the operation slowly found its way through the Chinese guerrillas in Malaya to Chungking and thence to London and Washington. There was no doubt about it. All seven ships had been sunk, a total of nearly 38,000 tons, hundreds of miles within the Japanese perimeter. Surely it is one of the most astonishing exploits of the whole war.

For the "Jaywick" party on the spot, the most encouraging reaction came from the Malay villagers themselves. Three hundred yards south of Dongas was the village of Patam on the northern coast of Batam Island. Soon after it was light, Lyon and Huston heard so much shouting and noise coming from this direction that they swung round and focused their glasses on the village. The Malays could be seen running up and down, slapping each other on the back in high glee, imitating the noises of the explosions and raising both hands upwards and outwards in illustration of their effect. It must have been the first time that they had heard such reverberations since the fall of Singapore and it could only mean one thing. The Allies had struck back. Scores of *koleks* started pulling out from points along the shore and paddling into the Straits to see the fire and the pall of smoke hanging over the harbour.

One such *kolek* caught Davidson and Falls unawares. They had made their way across the harbour unscathed, but the tide had started to turn against them and they were still about six miles short of Pulo Nongsa, a little island off the north-east tip of Batam, which they had hoped to use as their hide, when the imminence of dawn obliged them to duck for cover immediately. They found an adequate hide behind a strip of beach under some rocks and dropped off to sleep. Half an hour later they were awakened by the explosions. They were by now some fifteen miles from Singapore, and although they ran down to the beach, could see very little of the commotion in the haze.

They, too, counted clearly up to seven and wondered why the other two canoes had only accounted for four ships between them. Did it mean that someone had run into trouble? The fact that there had been any explosions at all seemed to rule that out. They considered every combination of possibilities but realised they would have to wait four days until they met at Pompong before finding out the truth.

It was while they were standing there that the

native canoe came round the point and caught them in full view. It was their first bad security lapse and entirely their own fault. In their excitement they had forgotten all the prescribed precautions, and if the natives had been hostile, might have had to pay dearly for it.

The sight of two bearded white men with their hands on their pistols was altogether too much for the simple villagers. It did not require much deduction for them to associate these two interlopers with the uproar in the Roads. Spinning round in their *kolek*, they paddled back like furies round the point again.

The question now was what to do. Should they risk a day passage to a new hide and probably run into further trouble or should they assume that the obviously terrified Malays would consider discretion the better part of valour and take no direct action? Their hide was in a fairly desolate part of Batam Island and it was extremely unlikely that there would be telephones or any such modern devices by which to report their presence to the garrison. The nearest centre of consequence was probably several hours' paddling away, so Davidson and Falls decided to stick it out. They spent an uneasy day at the alert among the boulders and, as night fell again, thankfully launched their folboat and started on their "forced march" south.

Hugging the eastern shore of Batam down the five-mile-wide Rhio Strait, they reached Tanjongsaoe Island, in the centre of the Strait, after nine and a half hours' steady paddling. The shore was uncomfortably congested with fishing huts and *pagars*, but they managed to find a serviceable hide.

The next night, that of September 28–29, they weaved through the maze of islands, keeping to the north of Pulau Lepang and Pulau Anak Mati, and then squeezing down the narrow channel between Pulau Rempang and Pulau Setoko until they reached the southern entrance of the Bulan Strait, a dozen miles from Panjang.

The last stretch between the islands had been the worst. The channel was extremely narrow and so thickly set with *pagars* that they had to pass dangerously close to the lights in order to get through at all. No less than six times they were within fifteen yards of the boat on which the lamp was hung and on three of them a fisherman was out watching intently for a shoal. They held their breath every time they drifted past, immobile, but they were never once seen.

In relatively open water again, they were paddling on their last lap past the point of Tanjong Klinking when they heard again the threatening plop-plop of the diesel patrol boat which had harried them round Panjang. Edging into the shallows to avoid pursuit, they watched the launch pass within fifty yards. They could see the glow of light in the wheelhouse and could hear the crew talking. It passed on beyond the point, missing them again. Keeping close to the shore for the last five miles, they pulled safely into Otter Bay about four o'clock in the morning. The dump was intact, but there was no sign of the other canoes. At the end of their tether, they lay down to sleep.

The other canoes had still not joined them by the evening of the twenty-ninth, so, leaving a note describing their experiences and movements with the stores, where they knew it would be found, they pressed on. It was thirty miles to Pompong and they intended to stage halfway on the island of Abang Besar, on the far side of Dempu Strait. It meant passing dangerously near to the observation post and searchlight on Galang Baru, but this particular problem was solved by an even worse hazard.

The sky was already full of scurrying clouds when they set off. They could see the great black pall of a "Sumatra" building up, and just as they were about to draw abeam of Galang Baru it hit them. The wind, waves, and spindrift had been bad enough in *Krait*. In a tiny cockle-shell canoe in the open sea it was terrifying. The only thing they could do was to turn the folboat's bows into the wind and sea, close their eyes against the battering rain and flying spume, and judge their direction by the force of the hurricane on their cheeks.

The hermetically sealed canoe rode the mountainous seas like a porpoise, sliding up and down the immense waves without once threatening to overturn. The battle lasted two hours, when the storm dropped as suddenly as it had come. They just made Abang Besar before daylight, slept off their leaden tiredness during the day, and by one o'clock in the morning of October 1 had the canoe safely hidden under the trees in Fisherman's Bay on Pompong.

They spent the day drying out, resting, and sorting

the new supply of rations they had picked up at Panjang. If all had gone well, *Krait* was to pick them up that evening.

From dusk onwards they kept uneasy watch. The hours ticked slowly past as their hopes sank. By midnight *Krait* was well overdue. There was no sign of the other canoe crews and the iron-nerved Davidson was just about to settle down on his groundsheet for a few hours' sleep, leaving Falls to continue the watch, when his sharp-eyed companion shook him awake again. "There's something moving in over there, sir," he whispered. "Can't hear a thing though."

With hope clutching fiercely through their infinite weariness, they tried to focus on this shadow within a shadow. It drifted nearer and suddenly there was no doubt. That long, low shape with the deckhouse covering the whole stern could only be *Krait*. She had come back and they were safe.

6

SUSPENSE AT LOMBOK

THE REUNION WAS TUMULTUOUS. FOR A COUPLE OF minutes, until Davidson hushed them fiercely, *Krait's* crew forgot their security precautions as greetings were exchanged and questions were shouted and answered. How had the attack gone? How many ships had they sunk? Had they had any brushes with the Japanese? But above all, first from Morris, worried about his beloved chief, where were Lyon and the others?

Davidson did not know. He and Falls had not seen the other two canoes since they parted company at Subar Island for the attack. After planting their limpets on the ships in Keppel Harbour, to the east of Singapore, Davidson told them, he had chosen to return round the eastern shore of Batam Island, down the Rhio Strait, and then through the "back door" between Batam and Rempang Island to Panjang. The other two canoes had been due to return on the shorter route through the narrow Bulan Strait, past the western coast of Batam. Davidson knew that the others intended to stay behind to observe results. Lyon and

Huston had the slow canoe again and Page and Jones were doubtless keeping them company. They could not be far behind and would be bound to pick up the message Davidson had left in the Panjang hide.

Quickly, he gave his eager companions the highlights of the previous fortnight, the hide-and-seek with the patrol boat, the abortive attack from Dongas, the long night out of Subar, and the desperate battle with the storm on the last lap to Pompong. Was he sure it was seven ships they had sunk? Davidson was sure, but they wanted him to repeat the details again and hugged themselves with delight.

Crilly pressed his special dinner in the willing hands of the two operatives and, as the excitement died down, the remainder lifted their canoe inboard and immediately started to disassemble it. The question was, what to do now? Although it meant postponing their departure beyond the agreed due date for the pick-up, they obviously could not abandon the other four without giving them another chance to make the rendez-vous. They decided to risk cruising up and down Temiang Strait during the following day and returning to Pompong again that evening. Meticulously, Carse recorded their dilemma in the cold prose of his log:

"We lay at anchor till daybreak, but no sign of the others. As we were directly under a well-travelled 'plane route, we weighed at 0615 and proceeded down Temiang Strait. We will then set a course east by south and return again tonight. It seems that Major Lyon is feeling the strain and as his partner, Acting A.B.

Huston, is the weakest link in the chain, he might find some difficulty in getting back. Sleep is the main need of all hands at present.

"While trying to break the anchor from the ground this morning, the hawser parted. It had been frayed by the heavy tide-rips during the night. So now we have no anchor large enough to hold the ship in a big swell. This means that we will have to cruise around all night tonight. As daylight tomorrow is the deadline for waiting, if they are not there tonight, we won't know what to do. The major said that if still alive by then, they would concentrate on taking a sailing vessel and making their way back that way. If he can't make it tonight it would be better to send Lieutenant Page and Acting A.B. Jones back to us to act as guides for us to pick them up at an advanced rendez-vous. However we will have to await the night and see what it will bring. I am too tired to sleep and the dye has brought out a sort of rash which is itching like hell. There is no wind and it is one of those hot, sticky days when it is uncomfortable anywhere you sit or lie or stand. The temperature is 92° on deck and 130° in the engine room."

Later, he wrote: "We are just cruising round the China Sea waiting for dark and praying for better visibility than we had last night for our passage up the Strait. Had the Japs been at all considerate they would have erected a few lights at the danger spots to facilitate our passages.

"After consideration it has been decided to postpone our re-entry into Temiang until tomorrow afternoon. This means that they will have two nights for travel instead of one and if we get there at dusk they will not have shifted as they only travel by night. If they are not there, we will run on to Panjang and see if they have received a message Lieutenant Davidson left for them. If they have not reached Panjang by then, we will, I am afraid, have to give them up for lost.

"Lieutenant Davidson is walking around with a *sarong* and a monocle, which seems rather incongruous but effective."

At half past eight on the third, after dodging several junks in the Strait, they were inching into Fisherman's Bay again. The scene of the night of October 1–2 was repeated: Crilly in the galley, Cain in the bow with the small anchor, and the rest of them alert and anxious, staring in the direction of the beach. This time it was Falls who saw the first movement. Sure enough two figures and one canoe were just discernible. Only one canoe. "Do you think it's the major, sir?" Morris asked Davidson anxiously. "We'll soon know now, Morris," the tall lieutenant replied in a kindly tone. He knew exactly how the Welshman was feeling.

The first pair was Page and Jones. They had come to ensure that *Krait,* in her turn, had not been taken over by a Japanese prize crew. Lyon and Huston were back on the beach with the third canoe. In no time they saw it putting off. "Hello, chaps," said Lyon in his brisk fashion as they came alongside. It was too good to be true. Everyone back safe and sound, haggard, stubble-cheeked, tired to the bone, but without a scratch on them.

Morris grasped Lyon by the hand. "Well done, sir, it's good to have you back."

The other four members of the party had stayed long enough on Dongas to compile a full report of the results of the attack. They had then made their way back with rather less difficulty than Davidson and Falls, and had made the original rendez-vous in time. They had been so blind with exhaustion that they failed to sight *Krait*. Their story is perhaps best told in Ivan Lyon's own report:

"At dusk on September 27, the party left Dongas on the return journey to *Krait*. We expected to encounter difficulties in the form of searchlights and patrols around Sambu but found that everything was normal. Arriving at the northern entrance to the Bulan Strait, we saw a small steamship lying at anchor. We drifted past it on the tide without being observed.

"We were all very tired and therefore decided to camp at the first suitable point. An excellent hide was found, which in daylight proved to be a Chinese graveyard. The following night we continued our journey without incident to Bulat and thence to Otter Bay, Panjang, where we arrived in a violent storm in the early hours of September 30.

"We had hoped to cover the first twelve miles of the journey to Pompong on the night of the 30th, but heavy cloud banks to the west indicated that there would be another storm, so we decided to postpone our departure till the following morning. To risk a day passage of 28 miles was a serious decision, but it was amply justified by the violence that later developed.

"We left the following morning at intervals of one hour and paddled all day against a head wind. Several aircraft flew over us without displaying any interest and we must have been clearly visible to the observation post on Galang Baru, but we arrived without incident at our rendez-vous, Pulau Torte, where we rested for an hour before starting out on the remaining sixteen miles to Pompong.

"Both canoes arrived at Pompong at 0300 on October 2 and circumnavigated the island in search of *Krait*. The agreed rendez-vous was between dusk and dawn on the 1st/2nd October, but neither canoe could find any trace of her in the anchorage. We therefore slept on the beach until dawn, when we stowed our canoes in the jungle. It was while doing this that we saw *Krait* about two miles away heading down the Temiang Strait. We then realised that such had been our fatigue on the previous night, we had paddled to and fro in the anchorage without being able to see the ship.

"A search of the island revealed traces of a newly vacated camp site. We therefore considered it likely that Davidson had succeeded in keeping the rendez-vous and, knowing the adverse weather conditions of the previous nights, would bring back *Krait* at a later date. Meanwhile we started to organise ourselves for a stay of several weeks in Pompong. Page started to build a hut and I contacted some friendly Malays, who promised to supply us with fish and vegetables for as long as we should stay on the island.

"They stated that the Malay inhabitants of the Lingga Archipelago were living in a state of misery, without any supplies of rice, sago or clothing. They further said that they had no interest in who won the war providing that normal trading could be resumed. That under the present conditions, the *bugis* sailors were afraid to put to sea, resulting in a complete breakdown in trade. When asked if it would be possible to smuggle rubber to Australia in return for rice they considered that the Japanese restrictions to navigation east of Ambon were such that this would not be possible.

"It was our intention at this time to pirate a native sailing vessel and sail to India on the change of the monsoon, but our problems were solved by the return of *Krait* at 2200 on 3rd/4th October."

The new arrivals had to face the same flood of questions and all the details tallied. The expedition had been a wonderful success and, when they heard how the Japanese search had been concentrated on the Malacca Straits, with only perfunctory patrols to the south, their spirits rose. It really looked as if they were going to get away with it. If the journey home was as easy as the voyage out, they were as good as back at Exmouth Gulf. But there was no time to lose. Feverishly, they broke down the two remaining folboats, stored them in the fore hold, and made *Krait* ready for sea. As soon as they had weighed anchor, Lyon gave the order to splice the main brace. With the warm glow of the over-proof rum seeping through them they all toasted their safe return, leaving Singapore, still buzzing like a hornet's nest fifty miles behind them.

Carse and the seven-man crew offered cheerfully to stand the next few watches so that the operatives could sleep off their exhaustion, although they were in little better shape themselves. The return journey along the now well-travelled route to south-west Borneo was almost entirely uneventful. They intended to hold on a little further to the east this time in order to approach Lombok from a different direction in the hope of exciting less suspicion.

With the tide in their favour, they were clear of Temiang Strait by three o'clock in the morning of the fourth. Nothing was sighted during the day except for a four-engined flying boat on a northerly course, which passed over them during the afternoon without paying the slightest attention. By now the six operatives were slept out and they could resume their full watch-keeping bill, which relieved the strain on everyone. The following day Carse was able to be a little more expansive in his log:

"*0600:* Sky overcast. There is a considerable haze and visibility is just nice for us. Most of the excitement has now died down and we are back to normal routine. The operation so far has been an unqualified success. All that remains is to return safely with our information. Everyone is impatient at our speed. The ship's company have not set foot ashore since September 1 and are feeling the need for some of life's little comforts and fresh food of a more satisfying kind than we are getting at present. Leading Seaman Cain and myself are suffering from prickly heat and two or three of the others have boils or carbuncles.

"One of the greatest shortages of this trip has been torch batteries. They have to be used continuously in the engine room. Our battery charging auxiliary motor is kerosene driven and uses quite a lot as it has to be running for one or two hours daily. We left Exmouth with three 44 gallon drums but are now on to the last drum. As we were so fully loaded at that time it would have been dangerous to carry more as they all had to be stowed as deck cargo. Another shortage is 24-volt lights, as in a rough sea they very often get a knock and are rendered useless. The only two left are in the wheelhouse. One is for the binnacle and the other on the chart table. The latter I have not used since we have been in enemy waters, but I am keeping it as a spare binnacle light."

On the sixth they passed through the Karimata Strait, and although they only sighted one sail all day, the sky was showing a disturbing tendency to clear. However, the cloud and haze seemed to thicken each morning and only dispersed gradually during the day. On the eighth they had engine trouble, caused by a fractured spring on a fuel valve. Paddy McDowell soon had this repaired and took the opportunity of changing the lubricating oil in the sump. The ninth again was completely uneventful, although the increasing head sea and wind reduced the day's run to only 120 miles. The next two days saw them approaching their final crisis. The indefatigable Carse calmly noted all the details in his log:

"October 10: Now that we are getting close to the Strait again, about 26 hours' steaming, we are starting to get that Lombok feeling once more. So far the weather has been perfect for us and we are hoping it will last for at least three more days till we get at least 300 miles south of enemy territory. Our trip back so far has been quiet and it really needs to remain so, because one and one only mistake means good night for us.

"October 11: We have all painted up again excepting Acting A.B. Jones, who in cases like this acts as a hand waver. He has the build of a Jap and somewhat the same colouring and is to show himself on deck and wave to any inquisitive Japanese 'plane that might circle round the ship either to-day or tomorrow or the day after. After that we shall be reasonably safe and be able to look forward to a good meal and a bottle of beer at Exmouth.

"To-day has easily been the clearest day since commencing our return journey and the one day that we really did not need to see at all far. As there is nearly a full moon tonight, I hope that it clouds over a little before we enter the Strait.

"We are now preparing for the worst that the weather and tide-rips may offer. We have two canvas bags to hang forward and drip oil on the troubled waters and one aft just to make assurance doubly sure. We will also batten down No. 3 hold, which is a combined wardroom and wireless cabin.

"As the darkness approached we increased speed to our maximum and drove her at it. A fresh south-easterly had sprung up and the sea was short and very choppy. As we neared the northern narrows we encountered tide-rips with the waves breaking all over us. This went on until 2300 when we got into the Strait proper and the water was fairly calm."

Half an hour later it looked as if they had fallen at the last hurdle. Lyon and Page were below in the cabin with Young. Davidson was tucked in behind Carse in the wheelhouse. Falls and Jones were on look-out duty on its roof and the remainder were catnapping under the awning aft.

With the tide-rip behind her, *Krait* was lurching and groaning ahead at several knots above her maximum speed. The moon was up, but low scurrying clouds made for indifferent visibility. Suddenly, Falls leant over and tapped his companion on the back and said: "What do you make of that, Arty?" There was something moving out from the Lombok shore. They both peered at it through their glasses, but the binoculars had been hard used during the trip and the mirrors were badly blurred with sea moisture. They stared again with the naked eye. There was no doubt about it, there was a craft making towards them on their port beam. From the big bow-wave she was under power and fast at that. "Go and wake the captain, Arty," said Falls, clambering down himself to report to Davidson and then running back to wake up the rest of the crew.

Lyon was roused on the instant, took one look at the approaching danger, and ordered action stations. Calmly, with Falls handing round their weapons, they took up their positions under the awning, peering out into the night under the covers at this last-minute menace which threatened to dash all their hopes.

Lyon came round to make sure that everyone was in position. By now there was no doubt that this was a naval patrol vessel of some sort. Would their grenades, Brens, and Sten guns be enough to deal with her? The sea was still running far too high for them to try their desperate tactic with the dinghy. It would never even get alongside. If things went badly, they knew what their fate would be. There was an emergency charge of explosive in the bilges, and if the worst came to the worst, one of the officers would go below to fire the detonator and scuttle the ship.

There was no question of surrender and capture. They knew too much and had done too much. The Japanese flag flying at the stern ruled out all question of their being treated as prisoners of war. They would follow *Krait* down into the thousand fathoms of the Lombok Strait. They would not last long. The sharks they had seen attacking the log on the way in would see to that.

Lyon squatted down next to his oldest comrade-in-arms and asked: "Well, Morris, how do you feel?"

"Pretty bloody, sir," said the tough little Welshman. "But it's not so much how we're feeling, sir, it's how they're feeling."

Lyon and Morris had been through this sort of thing together before, but some of the others were only eighteen or nineteen years old and this was the only occasion during the trip when real disaster had stared them in the face. They looked at the recumbent forms, each man quietly lining up his gun, and felt reassured. "I think the lads are bearing up pretty well," said Morris encouragingly.

Within minutes, their worst fears were confirmed. Looming larger every moment, with a great bone in her teeth, the ship came straight at them. If she held her course it looked as if she would ram *Krait* amidships.

Then, little more than a cable's length away, she turned to port to run on a parallel course off *Krait*'s port bow. Carse turned gently away on a more westerly course, just enough to show the tattered Japanese ensign at the stern. This was no armed launch such as *Krait* might have hoped to tackle on something like favourable terms, but a sleek modern destroyer or frigate, nearly three hundred feet long. She closed to within a hundred yards.

Afraid that the suspense might crack young nerves, Lyon spoke quietly to them: "Hold your fire now. Do nothing until I tell you." They were all out of sight, except for Carse in the wheelhouse, and they would have to rely on bluff. *Krait* looked her part exactly, a dirty, battered coastal craft, plying on her normal business between the islands. It was probably just as well that the new engine had never given them the turn of speed they had hoped for. Across the tide, they could not make more than six or seven knots if they tried and this might serve further to disarm suspicion.

With the destroyer beam on, they could make out her torpedo tubes and what were probably four- or five-inch guns fore and aft. They would not stand a chance. But as the breathless moments ticked past, nothing happened. No searchlight opened up, no warning shot was fired across *Krait*'s bows, no one hailed, and they could not see a living soul on board. For fully five minutes she paced them, until it seemed as if someone must crack under the strain. Then they saw the water boil again under her stern. Picking up full speed she sheered off the way she had come.

It was too good to believe. "No one move now," snapped Lyon, but the danger was over. As she turned, a light became visible aft and this slowly twinkled into the distance. Weary and spent, Carse turned *Krait* on to her original course. It was just after midnight and he handed over the watch to Davidson.

"Thank Christ that's over," muttered the usually irrepressible Marsh, speaking for them all. Lyon came round again, patting them all on the back. "Well done, chaps," he said. Morris nipped down into the engine room to reassure McDowell. "You couldn't lend me some toilet paper, could you, Paddy?" he asked. The old stoker glowered at him. "What do you want it for," he growled, overlooking the fact that this was the one commodity they did not carry on board. "What do you think I want it for after that little lot," Morris answered, and then they both laughed.

It was the most incredible escape and they could hardly believe that their luck had held. How on earth had they got away with it? Carse suggested some of the reasons in his log:

"Whether it was because of the approach to the change of watches and the officer of the first had had a big day and wanted to go to his bunk or they had got into trouble with some high ranking official over stopping similar boats we can't tell, but it was certainly a miracle.

"It was bright moonlight at the time and we were flying the Japanese ensign, which would have been plainly visible to them. This, plus our type of vessel, apparently swung the balance of doubt in our favour and left us in one large lump, safe and sound, although many sighs of relief were heard. At the time we were off Tanjong Batae Tega on a south-south-west course and all we could do was to alter course due west and hope for the best, and it worked."

Lyon was terse in his comment once the danger had passed: "If I was the Japanese C.-in-C. of this particular area," he told Morris, "I would court-martial without any hesitation whatsoever the officer of the watch on that vessel. Never mind how inoffensive we looked, had we been a dinghy we should have been intercepted and interrogated after what had happened."

They soon had something else to worry about, but this time it was only a normal hazard of the passage. As they started to draw abeam of Nusa Besar Island a couple of hours later, they hit the cross tide-rips in the southern narrows. *Krait* pitched and rolled as only she could in mountainous waves thirty and forty feet high, but by dawn they were through. As day broke, Carse wrote in his battered cash book:

"*October 12, 0545:* At daylight Nusa Besar and Telok Blongas were still visible astern and the sea still 6, wind 4 south-easterly. The sky was hazy with a tendency to cloud over. Well, if we survive to-day and tomorrow all should be well, but if possible we do not want another half hour like last night.

"*1930:* No sightings. We have just hauled the Japanese ensign down for the last time on this trip. From now on we once again become an efficient fighting force and instead of skulking by the byways and corners of the sea can now travel the main shipping lanes. However, it is a grand feeling to be free again on no man's sea."

The next six days were almost a pleasure cruise. On the evening of the thirteenth, by which time they were out of range of Japanese air patrols, they spliced the main brace again. The following day they had further engine trouble, but this was soon repaired, and during the night Young opened up his wireless transmitter for the first time during the trip. He tried to contact Darwin to announce their arrival but failed to raise the shore station. They did not want to run into any trouble from their own gun batteries at Exmouth Gulf, as *Krait*'s outline had altered considerably with the removal of the mast, and with the consumption of the stores she was noticeably higher out of the water. They had been away forty-eight days and had covered more than 4000 miles.

On October 19, Carse made the last entry in his log and signed his name with a flourish:

"*0200:* Came to anchor two miles east of U.S.S. *Chanticleer*.

"*0600:* Weighed and proceeded alongside *Chanticleer*."

They had passed right through the radar screen without detection or challenge. In high spirits they played one last trick. Climbing silently up the side of the American depot ship, they evaded the guards and were already wandering around the mess deck when they were stopped and brought before the commander. Fortunately he recognised them and grinned in welcome before sending them off to a massive breakfast. "Thank God you're with us and not against us," he said, "otherwise my ship would have been in a bit of a state."

Everyone in *Krait* had to be kitted out again completely. They had nothing with them but the dirty *sarongs* and shorts they had taken on the expedition, no identity discs, no letters, no uniforms of their own. The congratulations began to flow in, from the Governor-General, from the Commonwealth Navy Board, from Campbell in S.R.D. at Melbourne, and the party started to break up. Lyon and Page flew to Melbourne to report. Davidson sailed *Krait* by easy stages round to Darwin, where she was taken over by the Australian Navy, and Morris, his bad ankle still incompletely healed due to its constant immersion in sea water, was taken in *Chanticleer* down to Fremantle for proper treatment. The whole party met again in Brisbane, but almost immediately went off on six weeks' well-earned leave. When they returned, most of them were posted to a commando training school on Fraser Island, off Maryborough, in Queensland.

And Lyon . . . the first flood of formal congratulations had not led very far. He had accomplished this astonishing feat, but no one could think of any further immediate employment for him. He was almost an embarrassment, a standing reproach to those who had done and dared less. Too many "administrative types" had invaded even his own S.R.D. headquarters and he found himself engaged in vague liaison and training duties. He took over a small house at the entrance to the Hawkesbury River, near the original "Jaywick" training camp, and quickly slumped into a nervous depression, with the cumulative fatigue of the previous year slowing him down into one of his introspective moods.

But as the Australian summer lost its heat, his fertile mind started to tick over again. There must be some way of repeating the exploit, better mounted, better equipped, not organised on such a haphazard shoestring. The tide of war was turning too. The Allies were slowly going over to the offensive, and even if the main drive in the war in the Pacific was northwards to Japan, the vast area encompassing Malaya, China, and Indonesia still had to be liberated. The network of "coast watchers," saboteurs, and agents had to be extended until the Japanese were harried out of their ill-gotten empire. If he could not find further cooperation in Australia, he would seek it elsewhere, at home, which he had not seen for seven years.

7

"SLEEPING BEAUTIES"

THE DEVOTEES OF SHERLOCK HOLMES HAVE CHOSEN TO call themselves the "Baker Street Irregulars." It is a title that might more appropriately have been assumed by the members of the vast organisation which had its wartime headquarters in this same London street, the Special Operations Executive. The site is now occupied by the head office of one of Britain's largest chain-store firms, a far cry from the fantastic web of sabotage, agent-dropping, and assorted skulduggery on a world-wide scale organised from this respectable address during the war.

S.O.E. was very much a self-contained empire. It trained its operators, sent them on parachute courses, coached them in their cover personalities, taught them codes, ciphers, wireless telegraphy, and devised increasingly ingenious methods of sabotage. The organisation also invented and produced most of its own secret weapons. One of its most original purveyors of unorthodox devices with which to harass the enemy was a peace-time territorial major in the Royal Engineers named Walter Chapman.

A tall, gay, sun-bleached man with a bristling handle-bar moustache and an infectious laugh, he had made a name for himself with a Sapper squadron on special duties in the early years of the North African campaign and had then been transferred to Burma. Invalided home, he found himself posted to the S.O.E. research station at Aston House, Knebworth, another building which has acquired post-war respectability as the headquarters of the Stevenage Development Corporation. During the war it was the clearing house for research work on the hundreds of ingenious devices invented for clandestine warfare and sabotage in enemy-held territory.

They hammered out a wonderful gallimaufry of one- and two-man submarines, pocket explosives, ways of derailing trains, and means for short-circuiting transformers in enemy factories. S.O.E. amassed a tremendous archive of ground plans, blueprints, and technical specifications of industrial undertakings all over the Axis-held world. Scale models of them were built and S.O.E. operatives trained on them to plant plastic explosive in the vital square yard which would bring their activities to a standstill.

One of the problems in any organisation like S.O.E. is that the staff officers get to know too much to risk their being dropped in enemy territory, while the operatives, for security reasons, are only told what is essential for their actual expedition. Something of a barrier grows up between the two elements, as the atmosphere of life behind the enemy lines is something very difficult to communicate by word of mouth and the organisers on the staff often find themselves out of touch.

To help bridge this gulf, everyone was required to share the basic training as far as possible, and for this purpose Chapman was sent on a parachute course. He broke his leg in the process and when he recovered was posted to the headquarters in Baker Street to serve as the man to whom both staff officers and operatives could turn for advice on their technical equipment. He had a constant stream of callers, most of them quite unknown to him, recommended by one department or the other, and one day in the spring of 1944 the visitor's chit brought in by the messenger bore the name of Major Ivan Lyon.

Chapman had never heard of him. Lyon came in, taut, spare, with his small close-cropped head, not looking particularly friendly. He had even less time for office-wallahs than he had for regimental dunderheads and he obviously thought that Chapman was another of the obstructionists in the Baker Street warren from whom he had been trying to obtain backing for a second operation.

Something in his intent, reserved air immediately struck Chapman, who had been a combat officer himself long enough to realise that the chair-borne operate under a handicap in such company. "What can we do for you?" he said with a grin.

"I've just come back from an 'op' into Singapore, where we sank half a dozen Jap ships," said Lyon, "and I want to go in again. They tell me you might be able to help with some of the things we want to use."

"Have you, by God?" said Chapman, sitting up with new interest. Lyon looked up at the big wall map of the Middle and Far East Chapman had pinned up, as decoration as much as anything else. "Yours is the first office in this place I've seen with even a map on the wall," said Lyon tersely, but with a hint of one of his engaging smiles.

After that they got on famously. In spite of his brilliant coup the previous year, Lyon had met with nothing but frustration after his return to Australia. It seemed to be felt that the fabulous luck which had attended his first raid could hardly be expected to hold a second time, yet no one had been able to suggest a better idea than trying it again. Lyon felt sure that there must be less primitive means and equipment available for another expedition and had made up his mind to come to London to find out. He had made no attempt to hide his poor opinion of the "planners" in the Melbourne headquarters, and they, in their turn, began to find him something of a nuisance. In the end, they were only too pleased to let him go, if only to get him out of the way. Churlishly, they failed to justify a priority seat on one of the passenger planes and, in his usual tenacious fashion, he got himself accepted as supercargo on an air freighter which slowly lumbered its way to London.

After he had given Chapman a brief account of "Jaywick," they started to talk about some of the devices that had been tested down at Aston.

"What you want are some Sleeping Beauties," Chapman said.

"Sleeping Beauties?" said Lyon, nonplussed. "What on earth are they?"

"They are submersible metal canoes," Chapman told him. "We have only two or three test models at the moment but they are just what you need. Battery-driven, with a range of twenty to thirty miles. The operator has a skin-diving suit, breathes from air bottles, and can flood the thing so that his head is just out of the water or can take it down to twenty or thirty feet in an emergency. You can bank them like an aeroplane under water. One of our chaps has even looped the loop in one. All the acid came out of the battery, but it shows how manoeuvrable they are. You could carry your limpet mines on the foredeck and stick them against your targets under water. In fact yours is exactly the type of operation for which they are designed."

Lyon was all enthusiasm at once. How soon could he see a Sleeping Beauty? Were they difficult to service? How much did they weigh? Chapman showed him the plans and specifications and they arranged to go down to Aston the following day.

After one trial immersion in the clear-water tank they went over to Staines Reservoir, where two of the Sleeping Beauties were kept for training purposes. After a short course of instruction in how to work them, Lyon was clapped into a rubber suit and pushed off into the cold, murky water. He was a born operator. Within half an hour he was handling it like a glider, although he had been given strict instructions not to imitate the looping act of Sub-Lieutenant Riggs, R.N.V.R., who was the chief "test pilot" there. Lyon insisted on carrying out a simulated attack on the R.A.F. launch which was kept in the reservoir. He got right up to it without being seen and was fully convinced that the Sleeping Beauty was the craft he needed.

Thus began Ivan Lyon's second major battle with "authority." Not only were there no operational Sleeping Beauties in existence, but he had to start another fight against a world he considered full of obstructionists to get any sort of second expedition authorised at all. By this time he had more or less adopted Walter Chapman as an ally in what he regarded as the enemy camp, and Chapman, who was only too eager to get back on "ops" again, himself responded willingly. Lyon convinced him that there were often as many as seventy or eighty Japanese ships in Singapore Roads at a time and that if he could have ten or twenty Sleeping Beauties, each with three sets of limpet mines, the expedition should be able to sink most of them.

Knowing that a written plan is the first requisite for any military operation, they sat down together one day and drew up a comprehensive stores list, down to the last tin of "compo" rations, arms, ammunition, spares, clothing, sets of charts, and spanners, and started to hawk it around higher authority. Lyon was working on the assumption that he would be allowed to use three or four powered junks which he knew were being built in Australia in order to carry the operatives and equipment to their destination.

For some time they got nowhere. The frustration and

obstruction would soon have broken the will of anybody less single-minded than Lyon. Apart from the fact that there were no available Sleeping Beauties and no current facilities for making them, he came up against the security argument. They were secret equipment and under no account must be allowed to fall into enemy hands. At one meeting, with about a score of officers present, Lyon exploded:

"What the hell are you making them for then? They've got to get somewhere near the enemy. In fact they've got to get within an arm's length of the enemy, because the operator has to put the limpet on with his hands." It simply did not seem to have occurred to anyone that this was the case. However, when Lyon saw he was going too fast for his slower-witted colleagues, he took a grip on himself and did not press the matter. He had an extraordinary sense of how far to carry an argument without offending people and when to play it canny so that an idea could sink in.

He achieved his first break-through at tho Admiralty. He and Chapman went to see Admiral Servaes, who was the Assistant Chief of Naval Operations. Like many senior officers before him, he took to Lyon on sight, dragged every detail of "Jaywick" out of him, and immediately saw the possibilities. He liked the idea of another sabotage operation, but was even more interested in the idea of setting up a "coast watching" station on the Natuna group of islands, north of Borneo. Almost uninhabited, they lay on the route of almost every Japanese convoy and fleet movement between

Japan and Singapore. Observers stationed there would be able to provide invaluable information for Allied submarine and air attack. This would mean setting up a big stores dump, and Lyon asked the Admiral if there was any way in which the Navy could help to move the tonnage required. There was a slight pause and then Servaes said:

"I tell you what. I'll give you *Porpoise*."

Lyon and Chapman must have looked slightly blank as the Admiral went on to explain that *Porpoise* was a large mine-laying submarine, one of the only two Britain had left at the time, which had taken a terrible pasting on the Malta supply run and had come back to the Clyde for a complete refit. "When would you like to go and look at her?" he asked.

Chapman, not to be outdone, replied: "We'll go up tonight."

They dashed back to Baker Street exuberant as schoolboys, packed a toothbrush each, and took the night sleeper to Glasgow. Something had gone wrong with the train bookings and instead of a sleeper they found themselves sitting up in a third-class compartment all to themselves.

They were so buoyed up by their good fortune that they stayed awake all night, rewriting the whole plan of the operation round the enormous bulk of *Porpoise*. The submarine was to pack its mine galleries full of stores in special containers, dump them on the Natunas with a maintenance party to set up the coast-watching station. The Australian-built junks would sail to join them, refuel, and then carry the Sleeping

Beauties to one of the islands Lyon knew so well in the Rhio Archipelago from which to launch the actual attack. They would need to get dangerously close to Singapore to allow for the Sleeping Beauties' maximum range of thirty miles, but a forward dump of stores and folboats would enable them to make a more distant rendez-vous with the junks for the return journey. In their mood of keyed-up optimism, they even suggested a series of such attacks, with the junks refuelled and resupplied in the Natunas, constantly replenished by *Porpoise*.

Proudly, Lyon christened his second expedition Operation "Rimau"—*rimau* is the Malay word for tiger and the snarling beast tattooed on Lyon's chest became its mascot.

They found *Porpoise* in dry dock, a great bulging 1800-ton monster with an enormous mine gallery more than 200 feet long mounted on her pressure hull, obviously capable of carrying far more stores even than the comprehensive list they had drawn up. The Navy was wryly amused to see a Sapper and a Gordon Highlander crawling all over this great metal hulk, taking measurements, exploring the crew accommodation inside the submarine, asking questions about pushing mines or containers off the rails inside the mine galleries, and generally poking about, but the captain was much less entertained when Lyon told him that the Admiralty had lent *Porpoise* for a special operation. "Nonsense!" said the captain.

"I can assure you it has," replied Lyon bluntly. "Ring up my friend Admiral Servaes. He will confirm it to you." The Navy was not impressed. No one could ring up Admiral Servaes direct. It would have to go through channels. So Lyon grabbed a telephone in the depot ship and within a quarter of an hour had the Admiral on the line cheerfully confirming his intention. That put a different face on things and, after getting on good terms with such members of *Porpoise*'s crew as were available, Lyon and Chapman returned in good heart to London.

There they met a new crop of difficulties. They had *Porpoise*, but they had nothing to put in her. It would obviously take weeks not only to manufacture the Sleeping Beauties but also to devise and make the containers in which to carry them and the stores in the mine galleries. There was no question of retaining *Porpoise* until all was ready to be transported. She would have to make first for Trincomalee, carry out two or three operational patrols, and then proceed to Australia to pick up the party and its equipment.

By the time Lyon and Chapman returned to S.O.E. headquarters they were talking confidently about the "operation." They were more than a little dashed when the reaction was: "What operation?" So they produced the stores list and operational order they had concocted and insisted: "Well, after all we have *Porpoise*." In the end they managed to wear down the forces of inertia. By now the quiet intensity of Lyon's manner was having its effect. Colonel Davids, the head of S.O.E.'s production department, suddenly became converted and called a conference to tell his officers that they were to go ahead with making a sufficient number of

Sleeping Beauties. At last things started moving. They were completely unorthodox craft and had in fact been invented by a major in the R.A.S.C. It was quite impossible to go through normal naval construction channels, but in the end they obtained an appropriation for them and had them made by the firm of Fairmiles.

"By this time the thing had become legitimate," Walter Chapman recalls. "The operation was on, without anyone having actually said so. It was entirely due to Ivan's methods, I'm sure. Having got his foot just slightly in the door he was on the way to put another foot in. But I do give it to him that if he had not pushed it like he did, it would never have happened at all. He would go round talking to people, raising the 'ante' every time, saying 'so-and-so has agreed to this,' 'someone else had agreed to that,' and the thing gradually became an ascending spiral."

The containers were the next problem. They had to be about thirteen or fourteen feet long, the lower one wide enough to take a Sleeping Beauty with another smaller one above it into which to pack the stores. Fortunately, when Chapman rang the Directorate of Naval Construction at Bath, he was put through to a Commander Newton, who knew *Porpoise* well. He had designed her refit, knew her dimensions and her capabilities, and was able to agree the basic specifications for the containers over the telephone. They had to be watertight, able to stand up to water pressure down to two hundred feet when the submarine dived, and run on wheels so that they could be pushed out of the mine gallery and dumped once they had been unloaded.

The next snag was that the Navy had no appropriation for making such things, so the ever-resourceful Chapman turned to his old friends in the S.O.E. production department at Aston, who had blanket authority from the Treasury to make "containers." They were making big tins, little tins, crates, cardboard boxes, but if it was a container they were on sure ground. The fact that these containers weighed a couple of tons each and were made of half-inch steel plate bent round into a cylinder and welded was beside the point. The contract was placed with the Steel Barrel Company, one of the few firms able to master the appalling production problems involved. They went under the harmless code-name of "J" containers.

By this time summer was drawing on and Lyon had to leave for Australia to organise the operational base. He and Chapman made arrangements for the Sleeping Beauties to have their trial runs at Fishguard and enlisted the aid of the Royal Marines section which specialised in the testing of small boats. The Marines cooperated enthusiastically and readily agreed to appoint a liaison officer with Lyon in Australia. This turned out to be an immense major named "Otto" Ingleton, who in due course went on the actual expedition.

Not long before Lyon left, he turned to Walter Chapman at one of his farewell parties and said: "I think you ought to come on this operation." Chapman was delighted. He had hesitated to make this suggestion himself, as he was still suffering from the malnutrition disease he had contracted in Burma and for all his six-foot-two weighed little over nine stone. He accepted with alacrity. The whole purpose of his appointment had been to bridge the gap between the planning and operational side of S.O.E.

He was greatly nonplussed to find that the organisation was not prepared to let him go. "Who is going to do your work?" they wanted to know. "What work?" he said in effect. He solved the problem for them by finding another engineer officer to take his place, who had lost both legs in a commando operation in Italy. S.O.E. seemed satisfied that here at least was one officer who would not always be clamouring to go on operations, so they agreed to release Chapman.

He was left with the final nerve-wracking problem of shipping out the expedition's equipment. Shipping space was the difficulty. It seemed as if the Ministry of Transport had no control over the destination of a cargo once it had sailed from Britain unless there was an overriding theatre commander's priority. One pipe-line ended at Colombo and India, but the Australian pipe-line started from America. At one juncture Chapman tried to have the containers flown out, but they were too heavy for most of the aircraft available. In the end the only way in which he could get them moved at all was to have them carried on the deck of the battleship H.M.S. *Howe,* whose captain was furious at the way in which they tore up his nice new teak decking while being loaded.

In the midst of all this planning and organisation, Lyon had been able to pay frequent visits to his family. They found that success, and the prospect of a further triumph, had mellowed him considerably. His sister, Ann Gordon, widowed by the death on active service of her Australian naval officer husband, found her brother more relaxed than she had ever known him and looking in some way larger than she remembered him. It was as if his whole body and personality had grown now that he had found his purpose in life. He had become more expansive and sociable, less buttoned up. He talked with unrestrained enthusiasm of his "Jaywick" companions, what splendid people the Australians were, and how much he was looking forward to taking more of them on his next trip.

He spent a last day with his mother and sister at Ann Gordon's home near Farnborough. They drove him to the station and as the train pulled out he leant out of the window, waved, and shouted gaily: "Goodbye, all, see you shortly. . . ."

On his way to Australia, he was assailed by high-command problems again. Strictly speaking, any operations against or in the Malay Peninsula came within the sphere of the Indian/South East Asian Commands. Lyon was going to launch another expedition from Australia, which was in General MacArthur's Pacific Command. There was still very little direct liaison between them, and Lyon had to placate both in order to gain the cooperation of either. Fortunately, after the experience of "Jaywick," Field-Marshal

Wavell was firmly on his side. India Command not only promised full support with additional supplies, but earmarked a number of Free French officers, who had made their way earlier in the war from Indochina, to reinforce the new coast-watching teams which were to be strung between Borneo and Singapore. One of Lyon's subsequent worries was that the ship taking these officers to Australia to join him was torpedoed by the Japanese and they were all captured. It might mean that the security of "Rimau" had been endangered.

To make up for lost time Chapman had flown to Australia via the United States, where he was able to arrange certain supply facilities through Colonel "Wild Bill" Donovan's O.S.S. The American counterpart to S.O.E. was only too delighted to help, as they were being rigidly excluded from the Pacific area by General MacArthur and even cooperation with the British was better than having no influence in the area at all.

Chapman also had initial trouble persuading the American Navy to accept the part to be played by *Porpoise*. She would be the first British submarine to penetrate the China Sea since the fall of Singapore. The Americans considered this vast area their own preserve. The only concession they would allow was that British submarines might operate within the 100-fathom line, leaving deeper waters for the large American ocean-going types. This was all the latitude *Porpoise* needed on her trip to Borneo and the Rhio Archipelago, so in the end no great problem arose.

The final hurdle Chapman had to clear on his

journey was explaining himself to two British security officers at San Francisco, who met his plane and demanded to know his business. Apparently they were being plagued by all manner of spurious Englishmen who were living on the generosity of the open-handed Californians on the plea that they had been invalided out of Dunkirk or the Battle of Britain. A long cable had to be exchanged with Baker Street before Chapman's *bona fides* was established.

To his surprise, he received an even more suspicious welcome when he arrived at the Services Reconnaissance Department headquarters in Melbourne. They seemed to think he was some sort of spy who had come out from London to report on their activities and gave him the cold shoulder. He found himself tainted with much of the hostility they seemed to feel towards Lyon, whose lone-wolf success and thinly disguised contempt for all headquarters staffs they resented. Chapman got away as quickly as he could to join Lyon at Fremantle. Here he found a very different atmosphere.

In the two months since they had parted, Lyon had worked wonders. He had encountered another wall of opposition when he returned to Melbourne, but in his patient, dogged way, persuading here, threatening subtly there, going over heads whenever necessary, had slowly fought for the men, supplies, and facilities he needed. His influence with the Governor-General, Lord Gowrie, had obtained the use as his secret headquarters of Garden Island, out in the Fremantle estuary, where he had been given a workshop company of the Australian R.E.M.E. and had gathered together the nucleus of his expedition. Only five other members of "Jaywick" had rejoined him: the magnificent Davidson, now a lieutenant-commander, still with his monocle and bounding with energy as usual, the perfect second-in-command; Bob Page, the gentle medical student, newly promoted a captain, and the three stalwart able seamen from *Krait*, Falls, Huston, and Marsh. Apart from the gigantic Otto Ingleton, the Royal Marine major, Lieutenant Ross of the British Army, and Sub-Lieutenant Riggs, R.N.V.R., all the rest were Australian commandos.

In appearance Ross was a typical university don. He was a gifted linguist, specialising in oriental languages. Lyon had selected him to deal with any natives who might be persuaded to cooperate with the expedition. In spite of his prosy exterior, he was a man completely without fear. Riggs was the cherubic sub-lieutenant whom Lyon and Chapman had met as the "test pilot" for the Sleeping Beauties on the Staines Reservoir. As soon as he had obtained an inkling of Lyon's plan he had moved heaven and earth to join the expedition and here he was.

For the remainder of his party, Lyon had been given the pick of the Australian commandos. Most of them were infantrymen in the A.I.F. who had volunteered for special duties and many of them had been "coast watchers" or had taken part in clandestine raids in the Solomons and the Bismarck Archipelago. They were the cream of the élite of the Australian Army, which made them by several lengths the best soldiers in the world.

Three of them were officers. Lieutenant Sargent was a typical outback Australian, built like a bull and very strong, a natural-born commando who would dash through anything. Lieutenant Carey was another outback type. Before the war he had borrowed some money and set up a coconut plantation in the wilds of New Guinea, living with the natives. Over the course of half a dozen years he had made himself a comfortable fortune. His chief asset was his cheerful ability to live entirely by himself and he was to play an important part. The navigator, Lieutenant Reymond, was R.A.N.V.R. Half Polynesian and half Australian, he looked like a Maori and had spent most of his life navigating native craft round the Pacific. He also had been a "coast watcher" and was thoroughly at home with the other members of the expedition, a contrast to his experience in civilian life, when his mixed blood had not always made things easy.

Chapman received an uproarious welcome, although as the evening wore on, Ivan Lyon, Donald Davidson, and most of the officers gradually drifted off to bed. He was left to face the rest of the party. "Apparently they had a sort of trade test for Pommies—or Pommy bastards, as you were to start with," he recalls. "The only thing that really mattered was whether you could drink or not. They gave you no warning of this, and there I was, dog tired after flights across the Pacific and the continent, faced by a contest in the consumption of Australian beer. It must have been my good night. Perhaps I was so exhausted that nothing would have had any effect, but I was the last chap left standing.

"After that I had no bother at all. Everybody did what I said without question and from Australians that is quite a good thing. It was only a long time afterwards I found out why. If I had not been the last chap on my feet I would have had a terrible time, but the others all fell quietly asleep and by the morning I was no longer a Pommy bastard, but a Pommy. In fact they had found an exact category for me. I was a Pommy Pongo plumber—an English army engineer. I had a name, I fitted into the pattern and was accepted, which was a very comfortable feeling because these were very reliable chaps."

He had one agreeable further formality. It had been discovered that he was not entitled to give any orders to an Australian unless he was a commissioned Australian officer, so he had to fill in an application for an Australian commission, which was duly granted. He is still a major in the Australian Army and has an Australian paybook which entitles him to a free passage back whenever he requires.

Training was still more or less theoretical, as none of the proper equipment had arrived. H.M.S. *Howe* had zig-zagged halfway round the world before reaching Colombo, where the vital containers had been off-loaded on the docks to await onward shipment. There was very little movement between Ceylon and Australia, and it was more by chance than anything else that a couple of small freighters arrived and were immediately requisitioned to take on the valuable cargo.

In the meantime the Garden Island party practised with their skin-diving outfits and became experts in managing their escape folboats in every kind of sea. Corporal Stewart—"Stewie," as they called him—the n.c.o. instructor, was amazingly adept. He could launch his folboat through ten-foot breaking surf and bring it in again without once turning over. The straits between Garden Island and the mainland were ideal for training, as there was a tide-rip very similar to the conditions they would find in the neighbourhood of Singapore and the Rhio Archipelago. The party became so experienced that they could navigate these flimsy folding canoes across forty or fifty miles of open sea and back again without coming to harm or making an error.

By now it was August, and when the welcome news came that the Sleeping Beauties and the stores were really on their last lap, Lyon and Chapman could hardly believe it. Their frustrations were not over yet. One small freighter put into Fremantle harbour with two of the "J" containers on deck. They could see them there but nothing would persuade the captain or the port and naval authorities to unload them. Their stated destination was Melbourne and to Melbourne they must go.

The same thing happened to the main shipment when it arrived, although they did manage to intercept three of the Sleeping Beauties off another ship for training purposes. They proved wonderfully easy to handle and soon not only the fifteen operators but most of the other nine members of the expedition finally selected were handling them like bicycles. The Australian Navy lent them an old cruiser as a target ship, and although the crew watched for the mock attacks with searchlights on, the Sleeping Beauty operators succeeded in sticking on their limpet mines nine times out of ten undetected. There were several hot arguments about their relative success, which were only settled when the cruiser had to go into dry dock. Her hull was found so festooned with dummy limpet mines, clinging on with their powerful magnets, that there was no further cause for dispute.

In the middle of this intensive training, Lyon suddenly developed doubts about the best colour to paint the Sleeping Beauties in order to render them as invisible as possible in the water. He enlisted the aid of a professor of natural history at the University of Perth, with whom he spent two or three days while the canoes were painted every conceivable colour to test their appearance under water. The professor finally decided in favour of a neutral dark green, and as this was the normal army-lorry colour with which they had been sprayed before shipment, no further change was necessary.

The only member of the party who failed to master the Sleeping Beauty was the vast Marine major, Otto Ingleton, who weighed over seventeen stone. The first time they strapped him in one of the craft it started to sink by the stern so alarmingly the moment he flooded its tanks that he had to be hauled out before he was drowned and the canoe lost. Frantic at the idea of being left behind on account of his weight, he insisted that he should be included in the party as junk master.

By this time the pattern of the expedition had had to be modified considerably. The powered junks under construction in Australia were not going to be ready in time, and the plan for establishing a "coast watchers'" dump on the Natuna Islands as part of the first operation was therefore abandoned. This would have to wait until their second trip.

Lyon, ever flexible in his planning, decided that the submarine should get as near to Singapore as possible and establish an escape base on one of the islands in the Rhio Archipelago. It was then to search for, board, and capture a native junk, to which the stores and special equipment would be transferred. *Porpoise* would then return to Fremantle to refuel and take on further stores, while the junk made for Singapore Roads. Once it had launched the Sleeping Beauties it would either remain in the vicinity to pick them up again after the attack or they would land the folboats at a forward base on one of the islands nearer to Singapore and scuttle the junk without trace. The attack party would then make its way back to the escape base in the collapsible canoes after disposing of the Sleeping Beauties.

In the meantime, *Porpoise*, at long last, had arrived. She had put in first at Fremantle, but the submarine depot ship which was following her had not yet arrived, so she made her way over to Garden Island and tied up to the "Rimau" party's little jetty, dwarfing everything with her huge bulk. Hubert Marsham, her captain, exchanged cheery greetings with Ivan Lyon and Chapman, and they got down immediately to the final details of the operation.

Most of the "J" containers were still on their way back from Melbourne, but the three or four they already had were enough to experiment with. Already certain serious defects were apparent. The six-inch wheels with which the heavy containers had been fitted had rusted up on the voyage out. They were oiled and buffed, but it was clear that the same thing would happen in a matter of days in the submerged mine gallery. It was also found that if they were tipped out of the mine gallery, the top was liable to catch on the opening as they tilted. The R.E.M.E. sergeant at Garden Island was therefore asked to weld on an extension to the rails.

Then Hubert Marsham had a better idea. Armed with his *carte blanche* from Admiral Servaes and already falling fast under the spell of Lyon and his enthusiastic buccaneers, he made the one suggestion they never expected to hear from a submarine captain. He proposed that the Sleeping Beauties should be loaded in the torpedo reload compartment. He would be carrying very few torpedoes on the trip, as he was under strict instructions not to attack enemy shipping, and there would be plenty of room for the metal canoes. Lyon and Chapman had always understood that no submarine commander would be willing to be caught on the surface in shallow waters with his forward hatch open, but Marsham had gained such confidence in them that he was prepared to take the risk.

This entirely altered the situation. It meant carrying fewer "J" containers, which could be bolted to the rails with a decent interval between them. Openings were cut in the sides of the mine gallery through which the remainder of the stores could be unloaded. The oxy-acetylene cutters of the R.E.M.E. company were brought into play and soon the superstructure had a series of ports cut in its side through which the stores could be transferred. For the unloading operation they had chosen a standard type of collapsible engineers' folding boat about twenty feet long. Three of these were mounted one above the other on the after mine casing, just abaft the conning tower. To launch them, a small party erected the sides once the submarine had surfaced and they floated off when the submarine dived again. They were then moored opposite the openings in the mine casing when the submarine resurfaced. They were built like surf boats, with steeply flaring bows, and could be moored alongside in spite of the obstruction caused by the enormous saddle tanks over the pressure hull.

During the first exercise the submarine dived, but the first collapsible boat was swept away by the tide in spite of all the efforts of its crew of six with their paddles. It was recovered hours later by the Fremantle lifeboat. They did not make that mistake again, and from then on they were always moored to the submarine by a breast line when it dived.

The "J" containers had another unpleasant surprise

in reserve. The first time *Porpoise* went out with them in position, she found it almost impossible to dive because of the air they contained. This was solved by half-filling the submarine buoyancy tanks with water. Then, after the first deep dive, they found the "J" containers full of water. The doors did not fit sufficiently tightly over the rubber gaskets. They had to bring a fitter over from the American submarine base at Fremantle, who ran round the inside of every door with a piece of chalk and a carborundum wheel. After the next dive they were bone dry.

Days of intensive training followed. The "Rimau" party became so expert that they could unload something like twenty tons of stores in less than half an hour. They tried it at mid-day and midnight, in fair weather and foul, until every man knew his way blindfold and his part by heart. Each container was clearly marked with its contents. This for the junk, that for the escape base, and so on. The Sleeping Beauties slipped out of the forward torpedo compartment like eels out of a trap. The stores in the mine casing included a set of sheer legs which could be mounted on the junk the moment it was captured to haul the metal canoes inboard. A schooner with similar dimensions to a junk was used to practise their transfer. The petrol-driven electric generators to charge the Sleeping Beauty batteries had been fitted with silencers which made it impossible to hear them even a few yards away. They had tried to think of everything.

As the training reached its final stages, two additions

had to be made to the party. Warren, the warrant officer in charge of the R.E.M.E. workshop company, had become such an enthusiast that he more or less threatened with assault anyone likely to prevent him being taken on the operation. He was added to the roll for the purpose of maintaining the Sleeping Beauties and keeping their batteries fully charged up to the moment of launching. Corporal Pace also insisted on coming. He was the unarmed combat and judo expert, so tough that he had corns on the sides of his hands, with which he used to break lumps of wood. He was too useful a man to leave behind.

It was the most lavishly and completely equipped sabotage expedition of the war. The six members of "Jaywick" could hardly believe their eyes at the bounty of it all. If only they had had this cornucopia at their disposal a year earlier, they could have sunk every ship in Singapore Roads. All the hazards of the approach journey and escape had been practically eliminated. *Porpoise* could always dive in the Lombok Straits if exposed to the scare they had endured in *Krait*. The attack itself would be made submerged. No longer would they have to hold their breath each time they drifted past a fishing *pagar* or whenever a searchlight swung in their direction. There only remained the folboat run between the attack and escape base. They assured their new companions that this would be a pleasure cruise.

The war situation had been transformed since their first raid on Singapore. In Europe, the Russians had reached the Baltic, the Vistula before Warsaw, and

Bucharest. The Western Allies had overrun France and were driving for the Rhine. Germany was being pounded into rubble from the air and two thirds of Italy was in our hands. In the East, northern Burma had been recaptured, the Americans had broken the Japanese island screen in the Pacific by driving them from the Marshalls and Marianas, General MacArthur had won back most of New Guinea and was already threatening the Philippines. Superfortresses had started to bomb Japan. A major sabotage attack on Singapore, the unscathed heart of the Nippon empire, might well finally shatter the Japanese morale.

There was one last brush with the Royal Navy before they left. The submarine depot ship had arrived at Fremantle and demanded the presence of *Porpoise* for inspection. The occasion was not improved by "Jimmy" Holmes, the R.N. lieutenant who had helped to develop the Sleeping Beauties at Aston. He had come out to Garden Island to supervise their final maintenance and had dropped only too readily into the free and easy atmosphere, especially in the matter of dress.

As the most suitable representative, he had been deputed to pay the respects of the party to the captain on board the depot ship. He chose to appear in an outlandish uniform consisting of jungle-green trousers, an American zip bush-jacket, a blue beret with a naval badge, and jungle-green boots. He was unfortunate enough to be received at the head of the gangway by the commander, "Crap" Miers, a well-known naval tiger who had won a V.C. for taking the submarine *Torbay* into Taranto Harbour. Miers gave Holmes the dressing down of his life, and poor Jimmy returned considerably abashed to Garden Island to report that he had received rather a hostile reception.

This was smoothed over by a personal visit from Lyon, but the outburst was nothing compared with that which greeted *Porpoise* when she finally came alongside, with the dozen ports down her mine casing, the rail extension, the collapsible engineers' boats on the after mine casing, protected by the new combing they had welded on. This was all too much for the captain. He demanded of poor Hubert Marsham what authority he had for changing the specifications of one of His Majesty's ships, but when the C.O. produced his orders from Admiral Servaes the matter was soon rectified.

Even so, it was necessary for Marsham to obtain formal orders from his immediate superior, and these had to be drafted without telling the captain too precisely what was afoot. However, Marsham got his engines overhauled, fresh torpedoes in his forward tubes, and a radar set, which somewhat mollified him for the clause in his instructions that he was under no circumstances to attack enemy shipping on this patrol, to avoid compromising the expedition. There was good reason for this. *Porpoise* would be the first British submarine to penetrate the South China seas since the surrender of Singapore.

The nominal roll of the expedition as finally constituted contained the following names:

Lt. Col. I. Lyon	Gordon Highlanders
Lt. Cdr. D. M. N. Davidson	R.N.V.R.
Maj. W. W. Chapman	Royal Engineers
Capt. R. C. Page	A.I.F.
Lt. H. R. Ross	General List British Army
Maj. R. N. Ingleton	Royal Marines
Lt. W. G. Carey	R.A.N.V.R.
Lt. B. Reymond	R.A.N.V.R.
Sub-Lt. J. G. M. Riggs	R.N.V.R.
Lt. A. L. Sargent	A.I.F.
W/O 2 J. Willersdorf	A.I.F.
Sgt. D. P. Gooley	A.I.F.
Cpl. A. S. R. Campbell	A.I.F.
Cpl. C. M. Stewart	A.I.F.
Cpl. C. M. Craft	A.I.F.
Cpl. R. B. Fletcher	A.I.F.
Pte. D. R. Warne	A.I.F.
W/O 2 A. Warren	A.I.F.
Sgt. C. B. Cameron	A.I.F.
L/Cpl. J. F. Hardy	A.I.F.
L/Cpl. H. J. Pace	A.I.F.
A/B W. C. Falls	R.A.N.R.
A/B F. W. Marsh	R.A.N.R.
A/B M. W. Huston	R.A.N.R.

8

OPERATION "TIGER"

"PORPOISE" SLIPPED AWAY FROM THE DEPOT SHIP AT Fremantle during the forenoon of Monday, September 11, 1944. The flotilla officers were not supposed to know very much about her destination or her passengers, but they sent out several crates of rum and assorted "comforts" for the hazards ahead. The submarine made first for Careening Bay Camp on Garden Island to pick up the members of the expedition and their personal belongings and weighed again in little more than an hour. Accompanied by the motor launch which had been taking part in the training, she rounded Rottnest Island and turned almost due north for the Lombok Straits after a cheery exchange of messages with her escort.

With fifteen Sleeping Beauties in the forward torpedo compartment and twenty-four extra "bodies" aboard, there was little enough room for them all in the crowded interior. The only way to ease the congestion was for the "Rimau" party to double up on watch with the submarine's crew. This relieved the pressure on the sleeping space and provided the unorthodox spectacle of khaki-clad commandos keeping look-out on the bridge or sitting side by side with the wireless operator, cipher officers, and engineers. Apart from playing cards, sleeping, or listening to music on the loud-speaker circuit, there was little enough for the rest of them to do.

At dusk on the second day *Porpoise* surfaced about fifteen miles south of the Lombok Straits. It was two days before the new moon and the only way she could buck the tremendous tide-rip was to go through on her diesels, retracing the route of *Krait* a year earlier. Even with her powerful engines, she still only made about nine knots against the current, but this was sufficient to see them through safely before dawn broke. Lyon and Davidson were up on the bridge with Hubert Marsham and in spite of *Porpoise*'s impressive bulk got a thorough drenching as the broken cross waves came inboard and foamed off the mine casing. Below, the crew and the commandos were all busy circulating "Lombok Snorters" to celebrate the first break-through of a British submarine into the Japanese-controlled China seas. These were pre-war Dutch guilder notes which everyone signed as a memento of the trip.

As soon as they were through into calmer water *Porpoise* dived, making straight for the Karimata Strait between Borneo and the Billiton Islands off Sumatra, which they reached on September 21. They had sighted three Japanese freighters on the way, but Marsham was under strict orders not to attack anything and, with a longing look in his eye, let them pass.

As they headed north-west towards the Rhio Archipelago they sighted a number of junks through the periscope. On the twenty-second they surfaced near one sailing alone in order to test her reactions. Taking *Porpoise* for a Japanese submarine, she hauled down her mizzen sail, hoisted the port registration flag of Singapore with the Rising Sun, and then took in her fore and main sails. This proved useful confirmation of the mutual identification drill obtained from intelligence sources and was duly noted as the procedure to be followed when Lyon's party had captured their own junk. After a cursory inspection through binoculars, *Porpoise* sheered off again and dived.

Her first destination was the island of Merapas, the most easterly in the Rhio Archipelago, which Lyon had picked as a suitable escape base for the attack party to rendez-vous with the submarine. It lies about four miles from the next island, Pulau Mapor, and is shaped rather like a fat sea-horse. The flat head, running roughly east and west, is steep and rocky, backed by a ridge about three hundred feet high. The curving belly, facing roughly south-west, has fairly deep water running up to sandy beaches, and the arched back, facing north-east, has three shallow sandy beaches interspersed with rocks. It is about half a mile broad at its widest point and something short of a mile long.

Porpoise arrived off shore at dawn on September 23 and made a complete reconnaissance circuit of the island at periscope depth. There was a coconut plantation on the south-western side, with two huts on the shore, to which two native sailing *koleks* were moored. This was the only sign of habitation, although there was a decrepit shed towards the eastern point. The northern ridge was covered with thick ficus and cactus palms, affording magnificent cover, and the north-eastern side was dotted with scattered tall timber and bush, interspersed with what appeared to be derelict and overgrown banana plantations. It promised to provide an excellent rear base for a large number of men, as there was nothing to attract the plantation tenders to any other part of the island.

As night fell *Porpoise* surfaced about two miles from the northern coast. As she closed the shore Davidson and Stewart hauled a folboat out of the forward hatch. This was only open about five minutes, but the two men had some difficulty in assembling the canoe on the mine casing and, after about twenty minutes, Hubert Marsham became extremely impatient with them. His batteries were getting low and he wanted to spend the night well out to sea recharging them. No submarine commander feels happy on the surface close to an enemy shore, and this was the first operation of its type that Marsham had carried out. Eventually Davidson signalled that he was ready, *Porpoise* dived to float them off, leaving them to make a detailed reconnaissance of the island before picking them up the following evening.

Davidson and Stewart had been launched rather too far from the beach and it took them one and a half hours' paddling against the strong northerly set to reach the steep rocks about midway along the northern coast. However, they found plenty of cover and slung their hammocks between the two halves of a dead tree, broken in the middle, which showed up very white in the black night in the form of an inverted *V*. This provided an invaluable landmark, which they nick-named the "hammock tree." "Spent a cool night. Slept none too well," Davidson noted later in his report. "The change from close quarters in *Porpoise* to the scented peace of this island was too abrupt for sleep. The scents of the flowering trees and lily palms was more delicate than any that ever came out of Paris. The sigh of welcome."

At dawn they set off to explore the island. There was not a sign that anyone had ever set foot on the thickly wooded northern ridge. It provided acres of cover that seemed to be inhabited only by flying foxes and a stumpy-tailed Malayan wild cat, so they christened the highest point Wild Cat Hill. On its southwestern side, towards the coconut plantation, there was a considerable overgrown swamp with abundant uncontaminated fresh water. Over on the northeastern coast they found that the abandoned plantations, overgrown with thick bush, contained wild coconuts, bananas, papayas, betel nut, and a busy colony of huge land crabs, who duly gave their name to the bay on Davidson's sketch map. It would clearly provide almost ideal landing beaches for the canoes. There were no mosquitoes, ample fresh water, and wild fruit, and the island obviously provided a perfect base, capable even of maintaining a "coast watching" party.

Not more than a couple of Malays were sighted down in the coconut plantation, and it was a fair deduction that they came only spasmodically from one of the nearby islands. Wedged between the rocks on the northern coast, Davidson and Stewart found two lumps of rubber, weighing about two hundred-weight each, which had been washed up and which they earmarked to take back to Australia when and if they returned. They were probably worth twenty pounds apiece.

After dark that evening *Porpoise* surfaced again about a mile off shore. Davidson and Stewart had no trouble picking up her bulk in the gloom and paddled out to her. They reported enthusiastically on the suitability of Merapas for their purpose and the order was given to start unloading.

Everything went like clockwork. Two of the folding engineers' boats on the after casing were floated off in quick succession, although the second of them had developed a hole about two inches in diameter from rubbing on a cleat against the one underneath. Otto Ingleton quickly patched this with cotton waste and little time was lost. They tied up against the ports cut in the submarine's forward mine casing and the transfer of stores from the "J" containers commenced.

Marsham got rather angry with the commandos for not tumbling out of the conning tower at the double, but all this had been carefully rehearsed. Every man knew his way at a walk in the dark and any attempt to hurry unduly would have resulted in someone tripping into the water. A couple of sherries brought up on the bridge soon induced in Marsham a more mellow frame of mind. All the base stores were out of their containers in slightly better time than had been achieved at the final practice back off Garden Island.

Then came an unforeseen delay. In case the submarine had to crash-dive, Lyon had decided that Chapman, Ingleton, Reymond, Falls, three of the commandos, and himself should remain aboard *Porpoise* so that in the event of any emergency they could stay with her and carry out the second part of the operation, which was to capture a junk. They could always come back to Merapas and pick up the rest of the operatives. This meant that the unloading party on the beach was about 25 per cent under strength. Although the stores had been broken down into handy packages weighing not more than a maximum of twenty pounds, they were having trouble humping them over the uneven boulders and up the steep rocks.

Marsham in the meantime was again becoming uneasy about his batteries. By about two o'clock in the morning he decided he would wait no longer and flashed a dim red torch at the shore party as a signal that they should hurry aboard. This was the one possibility they had not taken into account during training, but the alert Davidson, realising that something was wrong, gathered everyone together to return to the submarine. Everyone, that is, with the exception of the lone wolf, Carey, who was to be left guarding the stores until such time as the party either rejoined him in the junk or returned after the attack on Singapore.

All the stores were ashore by this time and a good proportion of them had been carried over the hill in the direction of the fresh-water swamp, which Davidson considered the best hide. There were about five tons of them strung along the track through the trees. Broken down into small parcels as they were, they presented no problem in transportation that an active man, even if all alone, could not cope with in three or four days.

They left him with a silent Sten and a revolver and he was perfectly cheerful. "Lonely job, which I don't envy him in the least," Davidson wrote in his report. "Good man for it though, and took to it with eagerness. I was extremely sorry to have to leave the stores where they were as it was not the best place for them. However I contented myself with the reflection that the place had been my pick before I had found the better one in the swamp. I am not worried that any villager will surprise the stores where they are—it would be the most bloody bit of bad luck—because there is nothing on the northern part of the island to attract one. The stores are well hidden, or rather, in good cover. What worries me is the time Carey on his own will take to secure all the stores in the swamp. Three or four days most likely, thus increasing the risk of tell-tale tracks over a longish period. Carey can well cope with the problem, poor blighter."

They all shook his hand as they left, wished him

luck, sank one of the folding boats on their way back to the submarine and the second after they had come alongside, and scrambled aboard. There was no visible sign they had ever been there, and a relieved Marsham immediately dived and set course for Borneo.

The next island Lyon wanted to inspect as a possible base for future operations was Pejantan, a lonely speck lying about halfway between Singapore and Borneo, within easy sailing distance of Singapore in the prevailing winds. If it proved suitable, he intended to use it as anchorage for the junk in the second stage of the unloading operation, to take on board the Sleeping Beauties, the folboats, and the remainder of the stores. On the way there Marsham, to his mortification, had to watch a large Japanese fleet tanker sailing straight across his bows, but although he started up his "fruit machine" he steadfastly refrained from attacking what was a sitting target. Pejantan was reached on September 26. It was a considerably larger island than Merapas.

A careful periscope reconnaissance indicated that it was completely uninhabited, with plenty of large sandy beaches, providing excellent anchorage in all but a northerly blow. By this time the morale of the "Rimau" party was sky-high, and a suggestion by Chapman that a group of large monkeys gambolling on one of the beaches was a party of Japanese submarine liberty men sent them off into the shouts of happy laughter such as only confident men can give.

No attempt was made to land, and they set off on their chief quest, which was to find a suitable junk.

Their optimistic mood started to evaporate. They had sighted several on their journey west, and a year earlier in *Krait* Carse had sighted a large number on the route between the Pontianak Roads and the islands south of Singapore. During the remainder of the twenty-sixth and the whole of the next day the anxious watchers in *Porpoise* did not see a single native craft.

In the evening of the twenty-seventh, to relieve the tension, Chapman started making a native "joss." He asked the engineer officer for one of the thick rods of brush carbon used in the electric motors and, after borrowing a set of needle files, started to carve the piece of carbon into the likeness of a totem pole, with a gargoyle's head and a spiral shank. When it was finished he put Davidson's monocle in its eye and Lyon's scarf round its neck. Every officer was required to put a finger on its head, gyrate round it, and chant "Find me a junk, get me a junk, wichety-wichety, bring me a junk." They all felt slightly self-conscious about it, but, never knowing what luck might bring, it was taken up to the bridge and duly launched with a strong twisting motion to send it on its important journey.

The following morning there was still no sign of any shipping. "I don't believe your damned joss understood English," Davidson told Chapman ruefully, but when in the afternoon they stood over towards the Pontianak River their luck did indeed change. They saw three large *bugis prahus*, heavily laden and round about the 100-ton mark, which were far too large for their purpose. Then, five or six miles from the shore, they sighted a smaller junk, about 30 or 40 tons, lying at anchor fairly high out of the water as if she had recently discharged her cargo. They all had a good look at her through the periscope and there was no doubt in anyone's mind that this was the craft they wanted.

As they approached, keeping a sharp look-out for patrol boats and aircraft, the crew of the junk started to pull up the anchor, hoist their sails, and get under way. It looked as if they had seen the submarine's periscope and were trying to escape. There was no time to lose. A well-handled sailing junk in a stiff breeze can outdistance a submerged submarine running on her electric motors without too much difficulty. Marsham gave orders to surface. *Porpoise* boiled out of the water and quickly closed the junk on her diesels. Ross was the first man of the "Rimau" party out of the conning tower and, running forward, hailed the crew of the junk in Malay.

The wiry don, dressed in his jungle-green uniform with a black beret, was unmistakeably European, but after the junk's crew had recovered from their first astonishment, they obeyed his orders cheerfully enough and secured the lines quickly heaved over from *Porpoise*. Then Lyon, Davidson, Ingleton, Warren, Cameron, Pace, and Ross quickly climbed aboard and *Porpoise* dived again. The Malay crew of the junk, reassured that no harm was going to come to them, willingly rehoisted their sails and course was set for Pejantan. The whole affair had taken little more than ten minutes.

Interrogated by Ross, the Malays told him that their *prahu* was the *Mustika,* out of Ketapang, engaged chiefly in coastal trade along the Borneo coast. Occasionally she would carry a cargo of copra over to Java and bring back a load of sugar, but this was usually left to the larger boats *Porpoise* had sighted earlier in the day. *Mustika* belonged to an uncle of most of the crew, whom they heartily disliked as a prominent Japanese collaborator.

Once Ross started to win their confidence, they told him of their woes under the Japanese occupation. Most of the village head men had been imprisoned or deprived of their position, and the population of Borneo in general was continually being ill-treated and cuffed by their new masters. The junk carried quite a considerable sum of money on board, the profits of recent cargo trips, and the crew appeared to take positive delight in the thought that their uncle was being deprived of this. Worried as they were about the fate of their immediate families, they seemed highly amused at the thought that they would in due course be taken on board the submarine and carried back to Australia, and readily spent their time teaching Lyon, Davidson, and Ingleton the tricks of sailing their cumbrous craft.

Mustika was more manoeuvrable than she looked. Once the latteen sails had been properly set, she managed five or six knots comfortably in quite light airs and was an ideal vessel for the purposes of the expedition. She started to draw ahead of *Porpoise,* lumbering along submerged in her wake, but at dusk the submarine surfaced, came alongside, and started to tow the junk on bow and stern lines. The junk's grass rope was not really strong enough for this purpose, and in the small hours the bow line parted. There was a few moments' confusion as the junk swung round through 180 degrees to come up with a crash against the submarine's stern. It looked as if she must be holed by *Porpoise*'s hydroplanes, but the stern line was quickly released and *Mustika* hoisted sail again and turned towards Pejantan none the worse.

On the twenty-ninth, *Porpoise* dived with the approach of dawn, but as the sun rose and there was no sign of enemy shipping, surfaced again and made straight for the island to ensure that nothing untoward had occurred to hinder the unloading operation. All was quiet in the sheltered bay on the northern shore, which had been chosen for the purpose, and a further reconnaissance round the island showed absolutely no sign of life. By the time *Porpoise* had completed the circuit they found *Mustika* already safely anchored.

With the attack stores, Sleeping Beauties, and folboats still to be transferred, *Porpoise* was faced by forty-eight hours of hide-and-seek. Marsham could not afford to be caught in shallow water with his hatches open and each stage of the unloading operation had to be cut down to a minimum expenditure of time. The submarine's batteries must be kept at full charge for emergencies and for this they could only surface for the prolonged periods necessary well out to sea. The junk party was therefore to spend the day of the twenty-ninth clearing her hold and generally refitting *Mustika* with the help of the Malays. As dusk fell *Porpoise* crept inshore again and, coming alongside *Mustika,* towed the junk nearer the beach.

During the tow the sheer legs and all the gear to be used for swinging across the Sleeping Beauties had been assembled, tested down in the control room, and checked by Ingleton.

This was quickly passed over, and *Porpoise,* after launching one of the remaining engineers' boats, stood out to sea again, as it would take the junk party three or four hours to erect the derrick. With her huge silhouette an immediate object of suspicion to any chance Japanese patrol craft, *Porpoise* must be kept out of harm's way. Any damage to the submarine now and not only the party's supplies but their only means of escape would be endangered. They had now been deep inside enemy waters for more than a fortnight and the tension was starting to tell. There was no point in running unnecessary last-minute risks.

Shortly after midnight, *Porpoise* nosed into the anchorage once more, with the first four Sleeping Beauties lying ready on her forward casing. Half the remaining stores had been taken out of their containers in the mine gallery ready for the transfer.

As she came alongside an altercation arose. The purchase for the derrick which had been erected on the junk had been mislaid. This was too much for the tidy naval mind of Hubert Marsham. He roundly abused everyone within sight and it took several minutes to settle the confused shouting match. The purchase had been Otto Ingleton's special concern, and while the party on the submarine was shouting at him to ask what he had done with it, he in his turn was shouting back to say that he had probably left it on board and that someone should go and look for it. It was one of those moments when taut nerves are stretched to breaking point over some minor matter.

In the midst of the turmoil, Lieutenant Langer, the navigator of *Porpoise,* went quietly below, found the missing purchase, and amidst a slightly shame-faced silence it was duly passed over to the junk. In a matter of minutes the derrick was reeved through and the work of transferring the vital attack equipment started.

Now that calm had returned, this went on with all the quiet efficiency of one of the exercises at Garden Island. Seven of the "S.B.s" were safely stowed and when, at three o'clock in the morning, *Porpoise* stood out to sea again to charge her hard-tried batteries, the whole of the "Rimau" party stayed on board the junk, packing the supplies in the hold, rerigging the halyards and sails, and getting her ready for the final trip. Just before dawn, utterly exhausted, they lay down where they stood to snatch a couple of hours' sleep.

The work was so far advanced by mid-morning that Lyon, Chapman, Page, Stewart, and four of the Malays went ashore in the folding boat to explore the immediate vicinity of the anchorage to see if it would serve as a future "coast watchers'" base.

A couple of hundred yards to the east there appeared to be a crumbling coral jetty. There was a little inlet by the side of it and, as the boat edged into the shallow water, a cloud of sting rays and brilliantly coloured fish leapt out into the morning sun to avoid these intruders. Several lengths of rusted rail leading back up the hill showed that at one time there must have been a prosperous coconut plantation on the island, but it had clearly been abandoned years before and, apart from a ruined overgrown hut, there was no sign of human habitation. Lyon and Page set off through the undergrowth to search for fresh water and gain enough height to see if the island was as uninhabited as it seemed.

Walter Chapman, ever practical, set the Malays to work in the coconut palms to chop down enough fruit to provide both *Mustika* and *Porpoise* with a store of fresh coconuts. Lyon and Page returned to report that there was abundant running water for any number of men. Apart from an ancient four-wheel bogie truck they had found tipped off the rails and a few broken bottles of uncertain vintage, there was no sign of a living soul. This was to some extent confirmed by the Malays, who said that they had never previously visited the island themselves and knew of no one who had done so. It was ideally situated as a special operations base and Ivan Lyon's face lit up as he discussed its future potentialities.

Everything had gone so well that he was in wonderful spirits. Every member of the "Rimau" expedition was fit and full of optimism, everything had gone to plan, and the special equipment brought all the way from England was safely in hand, hundreds of miles within the Japanese perimeter. The scene was set for a repetition of "Jaywick" on a devastating scale.

He sat on the beach with Walter Chapman, whittling away absent-mindedly at a piece of wood with his clasp knife, discussing the final details of the operation. They already had two days in hand on their time-table, and as the Malays had made it clear that they were not more than two days' sailing distance from the Straits of Singapore, he intended to lie up with *Mustika* at Pejantan for three or four days to give his people a good rest and bring them back to peak fitness for the final attack.

Chapman was to return in *Porpoise* to Fremantle and, as soon as the submarine had refuelled and taken in further supplies, return in her to Merapas for the pick-up. *Mustika* was to make for the island of Subar, directly opposite Singapore, which had proved such a wonderful base for the "Jaywick" party, launch the Sleeping Beauties at dusk, and either remain available to take the attack party back on board again for the escape or be scuttled after hiding the folboats and the necessary stores on Dongas Island.

In either case Lyon had no qualms about their ability to return unscathed to the rendez-vous. The pattern was so clear in his mind that he talked far more about the next expedition they would launch to set up Admiral Servaes' "coast watching" stations in the Natunas and Pejantan.

If he was over-confident, there was good cause for

it. Every stage of the operation so far had gone without a hitch. Their escape base on Merapas had been established in much safer waters than the congested inland sea in which *Krait* had navigated. No Japanese observation posts or patrol craft had bedevilled their approach, and *Mustika* looked even more unremarkable than *Krait* had ever done. There were more of them aboard, it was true, and although there was no awning under which to hide, as in *Krait*, there was still plenty of room below to accommodate those off watch. They were using a better dye for their skins than Lyon and his companions had tortured themselves with a year earlier, and their attack equipment and tactics were infinitely superior. This time the Japanese would not even see the canoes coming, or leaving.

There were certain additional risks. Moon, tide, and weather conditions were ideal just before the monsoon, and the Japanese, with shamed memories of "Jaywick," would doubtless be on the *qui vive*. The disappearance of *Mustika* on a clear, fine day must arouse some village gossip, which might well reach the ears of the Japanese overlords ready to counter the slightest threat of increased danger to their shaking empire. There were those captured Free French "coast watchers"—but then they had known nothing of the details of "Rimau." . . . Weighing the chances, Lyon was still buoyant.

Walter Chapman sat scribbling notes as final thoughts occurred to them, and then they eased themselves off the log on which they had been sitting, went down to the engineers' boat, and slowly paddled back to the junk.

Warren had been charging the batteries in the Sleeping Beauties, and so efficient were the silencers on the petrol generators they had brought with them that it was only when they were within a few yards of *Mustika* that they first heard the subdued hum of the engines. This was an excellent sign, as the batteries would have to be topped up again at their nearest point to Singapore in order to give the attack craft their maximum range. With fifteen of the canoes, each carrying three sets of limpet mines, it looked as if every ship they found in Singapore Roads was due to be sent to the bottom.

That evening the Malays cooked up a wonderful curry out of the "compo" rations. As the "tigers" sat wolfing it down, the comforting silhouette of *Porpoise* slowly drew alongside again. Marsham had drifted in gently with the evening tide and was delighted to learn that his submarine's huge bulk had only been spotted when they were within a couple of hundred yards. He had the remaining Sleeping Beauties ready on the casing and these were quickly transferred, together with the containers of limpet mines, the rest of the stores, and 125 loaves of bread baked by *Porpoise*'s chef as a parting gift from the coxswain.

The "Rimau" party had a gift ready in exchange. They tossed over sticks of green bananas and the great mound of coconuts the Malays had collected during the day. By now morale had been restored all round and the only casualty was Walter Chapman's little finger, which he broke trying to catch one of the coconuts. It seemed a small price to pay. *Mustika* had three weeks of provisions on board and there was at least another three months of stores cached on Merapas in the care of the reliable Carey. Long before these ran out, the submarine would be back to pick up Ivan Lyon and his party. The rendez-vous was fixed at Merapas under the "hammock tree" during any night from November 8 onwards.

Davidson, tidy and efficient as ever, had gone below to type the last pages of his report. It was his responsibility to navigate *Mustika* as far as Subar. Carefully, as if to fix the details in his own mind, he wrote: ". . . to remind me of rigging. Bowsprit. Forestay. Two shrouds. Fore Halyard. Topping lift either side, Spanish burton. Running backstays on fore and main. Extra running stay on mainmast, presumably as spare. Signal halyards on mainmast. Case strops on each batten round mast. Normal junk rungs and ferrels. Battens joined by light rope. These support weight of battens and take all strain off the flimsy matting sails. Sails with bolt rope on leach and luff. No time for more now."

The time had come for the Malays, who by now had entered thoroughly into the whole spirit of the operation, to be transferred to *Porpoise*. Ross had extracted from them every scrap of information concerning shipping routes and the control of sailing vessels in the Singapore area. They willingly surrendered their *sarongs* and native clothing in exchange for shirts and shorts and clambered down the fore hatch of the submarine into the now empty forward torpedo compartment. Their clothes would serve as useful disguise for the "Rimau" people who had to show themselves on the deck of the junk.

Then Hubert Marsham, the strain of his unusual patrol over, mustered *Porpoise*'s crew on the forward casing and ordered three cheers for Ivan Lyon and his men. The noise reverberated round the deserted bay, but presumably there was no one within earshot to hear it, so perhaps no harm was done. The very real bond which had grown up between the two crews suddenly caught at all their throats as the two vessels drifted apart. Walter Chapman had time for a last handshake with Ivan Lyon. "Best of luck, Ivan. See you at Merapas."

"Well done, Walter. Thank you for everything. Don't forget that hammock tree."

9

THE TRIALS OF *TANTALUS*

"PORPOISE" SLOWLY EASED OUT TO SEA AND WITHIN TWO hundred yards the vessels lost sight of each other. After a decent interval the diesels broke into thudding life. The time was ten o'clock at night on September 30. The huge submarine seemed strangely empty, and the subdued Malays were no substitute for the noisy Australians they had replaced. As dawn broke, the submarine prepared to dive. There was one last hitch. The empty "J" containers gave her too much buoyancy and their doors had to be opened to allow them to flood freely.

All the way back to Fremantle *Porpoise*'s wireless operators maintained constant watch for any signal from the long-range radio which had been part of the equipment loaded into *Mustika*. To avoid detection by the Japanese, any message would probably only come in one quick "squirt," but there was no real reason for the junk to come on the air unless anything went wrong, and Chapman and Marsham took no news as meaning good news.

Their own return journey in the submarine was

completely uneventful, apart from sighting a few sailing junks in the distance. This time they took the Lombok Straits submerged, and their own speed and the tidal set enabled them to make nearly fifteen knots. The night's passage found them well out into the safety of the Indian Ocean by dawn.

They sighted Rottnest Island at four o'clock in the morning of October 11. Four hours later, *Porpoise* tied up at the little jetty on Garden Island to unload all the personal kit of the "Rimau" party and take on the submarine's own torpedo reload gear and spare equipment, which had been stored at Careening Bay Camp during the trip. For security purposes every sign that *Porpoise* had been taking part in an irregular operation had to be removed before she reported to the depot ship *Maidstone* in Fremantle Harbour. This did not take long, and later the same morning *Porpoise* tied up alongside the large ocean-going submarine *Tantalus*, which had in the meantime arrived for operations in the South China seas. Walter Chapman and Hubert Marsham reported to Captain Chadwell, commanding officer of the flotilla, and were able to give a glowing account of the manner in which the "Rimau" expedition had been launched.

It had been decided in the meantime that Chapman should return in *Tantalus* to pick up Ivan Lyon and his party at Merapas. *Porpoise* was required back in Trincomalee for further mine-laying duties and therefore needed a considerable refit after all the indignities her superstructure had suffered at Garden Island. *Porpoise* could always be brought back for any major lift of stores to the Natunas to set up the "coast watching" net, although by this time most of the country craft being built in Australia were ready for the purpose. In any case, Lyon and Davidson would need a period of leave once they returned, before being in a fit condition to launch a third expedition.

Tantalus was to carry out a normal operational patrol in the South China seas with a full load of torpedoes, and once these had been fired there would be plenty of room in her for the twenty-four "Rimau" commandos. Chapman took a distinct liking to "Rufus" Mackenzie, her commander, who had brought a fine reputation with him as the C.O. of *Thrasher* in the Mediterranean. There was a very attractive air of cheery efficiency on board, and Chapman rather welcomed the change of surroundings.

He was very much looking forward to a few days in a comfortable bed, but was brought up rather short when he found that the guard would not let him out of the dockyard. He had never had a pass to come in, as the whole training period of the expedition had been spent over at Garden Island. If he had not come in, it was manifestly impossible for him to go out, so that he had to go back to the depot ship and obtain a fake pass to legitimise himself.

He only had four days in Fremantle, during which he teamed up with Corporal Croton, who was to be his companion on the pick-up operation. Croton was a sturdy dark man, another of the Australian commandos, rather like a Welsh miner in type, who had come off a big cattle station in the outback and was as hard as nails.

Tantalus sailed from Fremantle at mid-day on October 16. Rufus Mackenzie's orders were terse and precise. He was to "make contact with and to embark the operational party on the night of the 8th/9th or 9th/10th and bring them back to Fremantle." Then, in the hard language of war, his orders went on: "The commanding officer H.M.S. *Tantalus* is responsible for the safety of the submarine, which is to be his first consideration, and has discretion to cancel or postpone the operation at any time. . . . In the event of the pick-up party and the "Rimau" party failing to keep the rendezvous for the embarkation, the greatest caution is to be exercised by *Tantalus*, who should not hesitate to abandon the operation if contact is not re-established, or if he has some reason to suspect the operation is compromised."

Chapman was no man to be content with the role of a supercargo, and Rufus Mackenzie soon found that the best way of occupying his time was to give him a job. "He said the most useful thing I could do would be to keep watch," Chapman recalls. "They had a new sub-lieutenant aboard who had not kept watch before and much to his embarrassment found that he was only allowed on the bridge when I was there. It really was rather amusing as he was a young R.N. Dartmouth product, one of the relatively few produced during the war, and he found that there was a rather odd looking army type up on the bridge who was doing his job for him. I must say he took it very well."

Again the run through the Lombok Straits was completely uneventful, and ten days out, on the twenty-sixth, they made a rendez-vous with the British submarine *Stoic* about ten miles off the coast of Batang in Java. *Stoic* had been operating off Batavia and was able to give up-to-date information about Japanese movements. She had no unusual occurrence to report, and the following day, heading north, then west, *Tantalus* passed Pejantan during the afternoon at a distance of about ten miles.

Her immediate destination was the shipping moving in and out of Singapore Strait itself, and on the twenty-eighth, as they sailed past the island of Mapor on the surface, they could see the top of Wild Cat Hill on Merapas on the horizon. Early that morning they were forced to dive by patrolling aircraft, and when they surfaced again an hour later, had to do another crash dive when a two-engined bomber came in low to investigate them. No bombs were dropped and the bomber must have lost contact. Rufus Mackenzie decided to stay submerged for the rest of the day, as the frequency of Japanese aircraft patrols was not known. At the time no special significance was attached to all this air activity, especially as radio signals they received indicated that several damaged Japanese warships were on their way back to Singapore from the Philippines battle with the American Navy.

Aircraft activity continued during the two following days, and *Tantalus* turned towards Borneo to seek less risky targets. On November 2 she sighted a small Japanese convoy off the north-west coast of Borneo near Singkawang and succeeded in sinking the *Taga Maru,* a 3000-ton freighter. The submarine was hunted for two hours by the convoy escorts but no depth charges were dropped.

Tantalus then received a signal to take up station at the entrance to the Singapore Straits to carry out air-sea rescue duties, on the surface if necessary, for the raid on Singapore to be carried out by B-29 bombers on November 5. They were only just able to reach the area in time, as they were forced to dive on several occasions by aircraft patrols. They received no report of ditched Allied aircraft but were asked to stand by for a further B-29 reconnaissance two days later.

By the afternoon of the seventh there was no further call on the services of *Tantalus* for air-sea rescue work, and Mackenzie headed northwards to see if he could find any targets in the neighbourhood of the Tioman Islands. He was soon rewarded by the sight of smoke on the horizon, which materialised into a 5000-ton freighter with two destroyer escorts. While *Tantalus* was closing the convoy a Japanese aircraft appeared out of the thick cloud and the submarine was forced to dive. The aeroplane came so close that she could not possibly have missed seeing them, but made no attempt to bomb. *Tantalus* took up her attack position, but just as she was about to fire her torpedoes the leading escort picked them up on her Asdic and turned towards the submarine at a range of only 6000 yards.

Tantalus was in only sixty feet of water but went

down as deep as she could to wait for the inevitable depth-charge attack. Both escorts were now on their target and their Asdic pings were alarmingly clear as they criss-crossed overhead. Fortunately the nearest depth charges exploded not nearer than a hundred yards away, and although a certain amount of glass was broken in the submarine, they suffered no further damage. The attack was broken off, and as soon as *Tantalus* was able to come up to periscope depth they saw the freighter zig-zagging away to safety on the horizon. They tried to close the convoy on the surface, but had to break off the chase, as it had headed straight into an area which was marked on their charts as a Japanese mine field.

That evening Mackenzie and Chapman held a serious conference. *Tantalus* was due to leave her patrol to carry out the pick-up operation, but, as Mackenzie noted in his subsequent report, "there still remained on board 15 torpedoes and sufficient fuel and stores for another 14 days' patrolling. My main object being offensive action against the enemy, it was obviously improper to abandon the patrol in this state in order to pick up the party. In addition, the orders for the party were that they might expect to be picked up at any time within a month after the initial date, 8th November. For these reasons I decided to delay leaving patrol and carry out the operation until such time as fuel and stores and/or expenditure of torpedoes demanded. Major Chapman was naturally consulted and concurred."

Tantalus remained in the general area of the Tioman

Islands and on the eleventh sighted a coaster, which was sunk by gunfire. They rescued nine of the crew and the Japanese soldier carried aboard as guard. The Malay engineer spoke some English, but the halting interrogation of their prisoners gave little satisfaction. They had heard neither of any raid on the shipping in Singapore nor of the capture of any British party. Mackenzie and Chapman argued long over the possible implications of this, but decided there was no good reason why the crew of a small freighter bound from Kwangtang to Bangkok should have any particular knowledge of events in the Singapore area and decided to keep to their revised plan.

For nine more days Rufus Mackenzie tried to find targets for his torpedoes, standing first over towards the Natunas and then taking up station again in the Singapore Straits. On the last five days they were several times within a hour's sailing distance of Merapas, but, although they sighted possible targets several times, they usually escaped into the mine field before *Tantalus* could close them. It was not until November 20 that Mackenzie decided to break off his patrol and carry out the pick-up operation.

On their way south they encountered more interference from enemy aircraft than at any time during the whole patrol. *Tantalus* was forced to dive four times by inquisitive aircraft. These were not passenger planes, such as had been seen from time to time, but "Jake" float planes, which were known to be the main patrol type in the Japanese Fleet Air Arm. None of them pressed home their attack, and although it was hoped on board the submarine that this was the normal pattern of enemy patrol activity in the vicinity of Singapore, Chapman could not help feeling a little uneasy.

At dawn on the twenty-first *Tantalus* dived and approached Merapas submerged from the east. Moving slowly along about 1500 yards out from the shore, they surveyed the whole of Land Crab Bay on the north-eastern side of the island through the periscope. There was no movement in the scrub and abandoned plantations and no sign of untoward activity. Rounding Oyster Point, they closed to with 1000 yards of the northern shore to check the landmarks that Chapman had carefully noted during the cruise of *Porpoise*. The white inverted *V* of the hammock tree stood out clearly in the centre of the shoreline, but strain their eyes as they might they could see no one near it. This was nothing to worry about, as the "Rimau" people would be under strict discipline to keep out of sight during the daylight hours.

The south-west coast in its turn looked exactly as it had when Chapman had seen it seven weeks earlier. There were four Malays pottering around near the huts on the fore-shore of the coconut plantation, with one of their *kolek* canoes tied up on the beach. The broken-down bungalow with its verandah further to the east still appeared uninhabited, and the only change in the scene came as they rounded the south-eastern point, where there was a small bush fire burning in or near the old banana plantation. It was thought that the Malays might be clearing the area for fresh planting, but as it was in that part of the island furthest away from Wild Cat Hill and the swamp, where the party should be hiding, there was no cause for alarm.

This detailed reconnaissance had taken most of the day. Mackenzie and Chapman were perfectly happy at what they had seen and were in no doubt that Lyon and his men had made their way back to this undisturbed island. Chapman and Corporal Croton were to be put off in their folboat after moonset, about midnight, and the whole party was to be picked up after moonrise the following evening, about 1930. A fairly heavy surf could be seen breaking on the rocks on the northern shore, as the prevailing wind and set were coming from the north-east. It appeared as if the small bay just to the west and under the shelter of Oyster Point would be the most suitable place for the folboat to land. For the pick-up, *Tantalus* would lie off to the west of Punai Point, on the western tip of the island, so that the canoes could be launched from a lee shore and have the advantage of the tide.

Tantalus nosed out to sea again to charge her batteries and then, towards midnight, started to run in on the surface from the east. The folboat was taken out of the fore hatch and assembled on the casing. Chapman saw to it that a few tins of "compo" rations were stowed inside and that there was plenty of ammunition for the silent Sten guns that he and Croton would be carrying. Both of them were in jungle-green uniform with rope-soled boots and had big native *panga* knives tucked into their belts. The moon had set and it was a dark night, but the air was clear and visibility good.

"There's the fire," said Croton, pointing at the first distant flicker of the bush fire on the eastern point as they approached. It was difficult to contain their excitement. If all went well they might be re-united within an hour with Ivan Lyon and his "tigers," who must have been keeping a weary watch every night for just this moment during the past fortnight.

Tantalus rounded Oyster Point, and after a brief whispered exchange of good wishes with Rufus Mackenzie the folboat was launched from the forward hydroplanes, about four hundred yards off shore. As soon as Mackenzie saw that they were well in towards the hammock tree, which still loomed whitely through the dark, he gave the order for *Tantalus* to put out into deeper water again.

The sea was relatively calm, with a slight swell running from the north-east, but as they came within twenty or thirty yards of the shore the roar of surf breaking on the boulders became so loud that Chapman decided to bear off to the west and make for calmer water round Punai Point. This only involved an extra three or four hundred yards of paddling, and although they ran into breaking seas just as they were rounding the point, they were soon through it and found calmer water beyond. The canoe touched bottom about six yards out and was hauled ashore over a patch of dead coral and hidden in the scrub. The time was two o'clock in the morning.

They were not more than 250 yards away from the main cache area in the swamp, but Chapman had decided to keep clear of this until daylight, and he and Croton started to stumble along the northern shore to the hammock tree, which was the agreed rendez-vous point.

They had not gone far when they found that they had lost their land legs completely. The fore-shore consisted of piled-up lava boulders, anything from nine inches to three feet in diameter, all loose and slippery. Apart from four days' rest at Fremantle, Chapman had by now spent sixty-eight days cooped up, first in *Porpoise* and then in *Tantalus,* and the cumulative effect of this inaction was beginning to tell. Even the delightful spicy smell of the jungle, a welcome relief after the submarine stench of diesel, rubber, and sweat, was not enough to keep them going. They staggered on, helping each other over the worst places, but found it impossible to stand upright in the dark and were making so much noise that Chapman decided the only thing to do was to retire a few yards into the bush and risk a couple of hours' sleep.

They awoke at first light, greatly refreshed, and soon reached the landing point for the stores. There was not a sound or sign of any human movement, so they inched on again to within fifty yards of the hammock tree, got well under cover, and waited for the morning haze to clear.

Looking out to sea in the half-light, they suddenly froze. Not more than a few hundred yards off shore there were three large naval vessels in line ahead. They could only be Japanese. It must mean that the whole party had been discovered and captured and that when *Tantalus* came in that evening she would be in serious danger.

But as they looked again the panic passed. With light flooding the horizon they could see that they were suffering from some hallucination of exhaustion. The three ships were in fact three small islands much further out, the trees on them looking exactly like masts and the breaking surf exactly like a bow-wave.

"Phew," Chapman whispered in relief, "let's get on." Straining their eyes desperately, they looked for the shape of a hammock slung between the *V*. There was none there and there was no sign of anyone on watch.

"There must be something wrong," Chapman whispered to Croton. The corporal nodded grimly. "I am going on ahead," continued Chapman, "Keep me covered."

A few yards apart they crawled forward, listening intently for the slightest sound of friend or enemy. They could hear nothing but the crashing of the waves and the first bird cries of morning. Chapman stood up and started to search the whole area round the dead V-shaped tree. Under one bush he found a few pieces of silver paper, chocolate wrapping, but otherwise there was nothing, no tracks, no sound, no movement.

Tracks they had not expected to find, as every member of the "Rimau" party was trained to obliterate his footsteps with a little wire brush, but the silence was uncanny and menacing. Knowing Lyon's iron standards of discipline, Chapman could not believe that careless watch was being kept, but he decided that the only thing to do was to go and search the cache area on the other side of the hill to see if the party for some reason was concentrated there.

The hill behind the hammock tree was almost vertical, but rather than use the obvious route from the landing point Chapman decided to scale it. They managed to haul themselves up by hanging on to the roots of bushes and the branches of trees. Suddenly Chapman's feet gave way. He had dislodged a large rock, which crashed down to the beach with an appalling noise, just missing Croton, but although a few birds rose in alarm, there was no further reaction. After a breathless pause they started to inch upwards again and soon came to easier ground and found themselves on the crest of the ridge.

The jungle of palm trees and various bushes and creepers was nowhere impenetrable and they were able to search the ridge from Wild Cat Hill to the west without undue difficulty. They found three unmistakeable tracks running across it from north to south, but none of them looked as if it had been used for weeks. There was nothing for it, they must get down the southern slope of the ridge and search the swamp.

Just as they were about to start, a thin pi-dog trotted out from the other side of a small clearing. It sniffed at them and then sidled off again without making any sound. Unless it was completely wild, it probably came from the Malay huts down on the south-west shore, and the fact that it seemed unperturbed by their presence might indicate that it was not surprised at finding strangers on its morning walk. Walter Chapman's spirits rose again, but just to make sure that they were in a position to defend themselves in case of trouble, he and Croton fired off a few rounds out of their silent Stens to clear the barrels. The faint clicking noise did not even alarm the birds.

With Croton covering him from behind, Chapman started to walk down through the bush, parallel to the disused Malay path which appeared to lead down to the junction of the coconut plantation and the swamp area. Still finding nothing, Chapman took stock. The situation was clearly a dangerous one. Apart from the Malays they knew to be in their huts on the south-west shore, there was no sign of human activity, but it might be wise to ensure that their own line of retreat was secure. They therefore worked their way along the northern fringe of the swamp to their canoe hide to make sure that the folboat had been properly concealed against prying eyes in daylight. They found it where they had left it, and after pulling the canoe a few yards further into the undergrowth, retraced their steps.

This time they started into the swamp area itself. They soon found two water holes which had been dug. At the edge of the first was an empty ration tin and the lid of a dixie, which had clearly been used as balers. On a branch of the tree above they found a sweat rag and a bandage. At the second hole they found two further baling tins made out of "compo"-ration tins cut in half, diagonally. There were no footprints and the earth had been washed smooth, probably an indication of recent rains.

From the water hole a recognisable path led uphill

again towards the ridge. This they followed and after a sharp turn to the east came into a fair-sized clearing with a large lean-to shelter, about twenty-five feet long and ten feet wide, with an interlaced palm-leaf covering and a palm-leaf-covered floor. It was totally deserted, but with ample evidence of recent occupation. Food cooking in tins had been left undisturbed, the fires apparently kicked out. There were half a dozen large "compo"-ration tins lying about, empty, but with the base A markings still on them and twenty or thirty smaller tins.

Feverishly the two men searched further for more evidence of what might have happened to the party. The collected debris only served to confuse them. They found a broken drinking bowl such as had been owned by the Malay crew of *Mustika* and some of the poor-quality grass line used in her rigging. This was odd, as it had been no part of the original plan for the junk to call back at Merapas. There were three or four lengths of the cord which had been used as carrying handles for the kerosene tins, an oil can which was recognisably part of the maintenance kit of a Sleeping Beauty, and the top of a container such as might have been brought ashore by Davidson in his first folboat reconnaissance of the island from *Porpoise.* They found two empty cardboard cigarette packets of Three Castles cigarettes, which had formed part of the ship's stores in *Porpoise* and which someone in the "Rimau" party must have brought off with him.

Then Chapman pounced on an object lying half hidden in the grass. This was the small cane rake which Davidson had made for use on the "Jaywick" expedition to obliterate his footprints. It was unmistakeably his and there was not another like it in the party. This could only mean that Davidson had got back to Merapas, but where was he? It was against all their training to leave debris of any sort, and in this respect Davidson had been the most rigid disciplinarian of them all.

The remaining finds carried a much more sinister message. There was a cotton name tag with Japanese characters written on it in ink, a large hemispherical beaten-iron bowl about two and a half feet in diameter and weighing a good hundredweight, filled with stagnant water, which was certainly no part either of the junk's or the expedition's equipment, and a sign carved in what looked like Japanese characters on one of the trees. Strewn around was a bunch of bananas, cut approximately a fortnight earlier and just ripening, two or three coconuts in the same condition, and some pawpaws, most of them rotten.

This was baffling. Some of the "Rimau" party had clearly been on the island to rejoin Carey. The food and commando cookers were recognisably part of the stores. But then who had built the shelter? It looked like native or possibly Japanese work. Carey might have learnt the trick during his long years in the islands, but it seemed a large structure for one man to have put up. And why the sudden departure with the food, now rotten and mildewed, left cooking in the tins. Had they all been wiped out? There was no sign of a struggle, no bullet marks on trees, no graves, no corpses, no clothing, no real clue.

Chapman and Croton sat down to discuss what they should do. By now they felt reasonably safe. There was no sign of movement on the island, no fires, and if any Japanese had been there, they had clearly gone again. Lyon, Davidson, Page, and their assorted crew of tough cut-throats would never have given up without a fight, yet there was no sign of it. It looked as if the junk had called at the island at some stage. Had they returned in it from the raid, found their hiding place compromised, and sailed on? There was no mark, no message, nothing to go on at all.

In any case, where was the main cache of stores? Carey had been put ashore with something like five tons of provisions and equipment, but it had vanished.

With sinking hearts and fading hope, the two men started to track the entire length and breadth of the island for some sign of the party or clue as to what had happened. They followed three faint tracks over the crest of the ridge to the northern coast again but found nothing. They then worked their way along the right-angled extension of the ridge down to the south-eastern tip of the island, exploring the gullies and beating through the abandoned coconut and banana plantations. They found that the bush fire they had seen had burnt itself out, but no sign that it was man-made. It was hot and exhausting work in the thick undergrowth and several times they had to pause, panting, to recoup their rapidly fading strength. Slowly and wearily they worked their way back through the scattered tall timber on the south-western slopes, with the coconut plantation clear in view and occasional glimpses in the distance of the Malays tending it.

Skirting the plantation, they plunged back into the swamp again. They soon found another eight smaller one-man shelters, each with commando cookers containing half-cooked food over extinguished wood fires, and another dozen small empty tins of "compo" rations. There was still no sign of the dump of stores and this was where it should have been.

Two of the shelters with inter-leaved palm-leaf roofs were built low to the ground and looked as if they might have served to protect folboats. The others, with four ridge-poles, might each have served to sling a single hammock and looked like the work of members of the "Rimau" party.

Squatting down, baffled and exhausted, Chapman and Croton discussed whether they should approach the Malay huts and try to carry off one of the natives for interrogation. They would just be able to squeeze him in the folboat in which they would go out to meet *Tantalus* after night fell. In the end they dropped the idea, as if one of them escaped he might well be able to summon help, including a detachment of Japanese, from one of the neighbouring islands.

Nowhere had they found any signs of a skirmish or Japanese occupation. There was even a huge hornets' nest near one of the shelters in the swamp, with the great black-and-yellow insects buzzing entirely undisturbed. The only sign of Japanese activity had been a "Jake" seaplane winging across the island, apparently on a set course, during the latter part of the morning.

"What about all that stuff lying round the shelters?" Croton wanted to know. "Ought we to take that off as evidence?" Chapman decided against it. He had taken a careful note of everything they had found and it seemed much better to leave the camp sites as they had found them in case the Japanese should come back and find evidence that a new party had visited them.

Leaden-hearted and utterly at a loss as to what to do, they made their way back to the folboat hide to await the arrival of *Tantalus.* There should be no difficulty in spotting the submarine. The moon rose bright and they could see for miles. They were still straining their ears and eyes at ten o'clock when Chapman sniffed the air and said: "Here she comes. That must be her." They still could not see *Tantalus* but his nose had caught the unmistakeable sour smell which is part of a submariner's life. They soon spotted her silhouette drifting round Punai Point, ran the folboat down the beach, and climbed in.

Rufus Mackenzie had brought in *Tantalus* with the crew at diving stations. He had been through a worrying time during the previous twenty-four hours and was greatly relieved when the look-out spotted the folboat coming out, as he had feared the worst. At dawn, while heading away from Merapas, *Tantalus* had been sighted by a destroyer or escort vessel, fired on, and forced to dive, although they had managed to evade the subsequent Asdic search. Two hours later, when they surfaced, they immediately had to dive again when they saw a float plane on the horizon.

They had spent almost the whole day continuously submerged, picking up constant air patrols through the periscope. The situation looked bad and the delays had made them late for the rendez-vous, as the submarine had been obliged to spend three hours out to sea recharging batteries as soon as dusk fell. There had been a further scare when the submarine spotted what looked like a patrol boat lying off Merapas to the south, but it had moved off to the south-east, and disappeared from view.

A considerable swell had risen, threatening the approaching monsoon, and Chapman and the corporal had great difficulty in coming alongside with the folboat. One uncontrollable lurch against the port hydroplane almost put them under, but they managed to clamber aboard and haul up the canoe on the forward casing. Rufus Mackenzie welcomed them anxiously: "Are the rest of your people all right?" he asked.

"I don't know what has happened," Chapman answered, and gave him a full account of their fruitless day-long search. It sounded ominous to Mackenzie. "It doesn't look too good, does it?" he said. "Perhaps we ought to have put in on the eighth. They might still have been there." Chapman had been haunted by the thought all day, but there was no way of telling. *Tantalus* might have run into real trouble if her experiences of the last two days were anything to go by. One thing seemed certain. There was no point in lingering near Merapas. If the "Rimau" party had ever been there in force, they had left days before and might by now be anywhere in the South China seas if they were still alive.

Any further search would almost inevitably result in the loss of *Tantalus* herself. Reluctantly, Mackenzie and Chapman agreed that the pick-up operation would have to be called off. Tough and resilient as they were, Lyon and his men might well hold out for months. There was always the possibility that they had captured another junk and would find their own way home. Haggard with worry, Chapman handed over wordlessly the bunch of ripening bananas he had brought off from the island, and the submarine drew slowly out to sea. The folboat was stowed down the forward hatch and *Tantalus* set course for home and safety.

"It was a very bitter disappointment to Major Chapman and a blow to us all," wrote the Commander in his report. "It is to be hoped that the delay in carrying out the operation was not the cause for the loss of this gallant party, but it is, unfortunately, very possible."

Tantalus still had several days in hand and looked for further Japanese ships to sink south of the Karimata Islands. One unsuccessful attack was carried out on a small convoy and then on the twenty-ninth the submarine headed for the Lombok Straits. There were no further incidents and she tied up alongside the depot ship *Maidstone* at Fremantle on December 6. She had been on patrol for 53 days and covered 11,600 miles, an endurance record for a British submarine.

All the way back Chapman racked his brain as to what might have happened. It was possible that Carey had been discovered by the Malay plantation tenders and the alarm given to the Japanese, who might have consumed some of the stores, removed the rest, and picked off the attack party as they returned from Singapore. The shelters might have been put up by a temporary Japanese garrison. But against that was the finding of Davidson's rake and evidence that *Mustika* had at some time called at the island.

The abandoned food in the cookers indicated strongly that the whole party had been surprised while waiting for *Tantalus*, but there had been absolutely no sign of a skirmish, no spent cartridges had been found, and there were no bodies or evidence of burial. There was no reason to suppose that *Mustika* had lifted off Carey and all the stores to establish base on another island. They would certainly never have left the Merapas base in such a condition. Merapas might have been compromised as a rendez-vous and the party hiding on another island, but in that case they would have risked almost anything to leave either a message or a watch at the hammock tree, and there had been no sign of either.

Japanese air and sea patrol activity during the two days that *Tantalus* had been in the vicinity of Merapas was a very bad sign, but this still did not explain the fact that the island appeared completely undisturbed with the Malays in the coconut plantation going about their normal business totally unconcerned. Who had brought the heavy iron cooking bowl and manhandled it halfway up a 300-foot hill? Why had it been abandoned?

Something had clearly gone badly wrong with operation "Rimau." The name tag that Chapman had brought back spelt out the name Takahiro Watanabe, which was obviously Japanese. The sign carved on the tree, of which he had taken a copy, proved to be the character for Japan and had been carved or daubed along their path all over South East Asia by the soldiers of the Rising Sun. Careful reading of Japanese wireless intercepts over the succeeding weeks seemed to indicate that there had been a brush of some sort with an Allied party in the Singapore area. The mystery was not solved until the war in the Far East was over.

10

SEQUEL AT SINGKEP

EVEN IF "TANTALUS" HAD REACHED MERAPAS ON THE first rendez-vous night, November 8, she would not have been able to carry out the pick-up and might well have been sunk herself. By that time Lyon, Davidson, Ross, and at least three of the Australian commandos were dead. The remainder, if the confused dates of the Japanese records can be reconciled, were still alive, but scattered in twos and threes far to the south in the Lingga Archipelago, hunted and desperate. *Mustika* had been challenged within a dozen miles of Singapore and the expedition had been abandoned. With "Jaywick" to avenge, the Japanese had set every available plane, patrol boat, and soldier to round up these impudent intruders.

When the Japanese empire surrendered in the autumn of 1945, the Allies faced the mountainous task of tracing their prisoners of war and compiling evidence on which to try the perpetrators of the holocaust of atrocities to which soldier, native, and civilian internee had been subjected. In Singapore and Malaya, the task was gargantuan. Thousands of P.O.W.'s had died on the infamous Siam railway, further thousands of Malays and Chinese had been slaughtered or starved to death in stinking gaols, Europeans had been beaten, tortured, executed on trumped-up charges in their scores. Records had been destroyed, vital witnesses had disappeared, and the Japanese, arrogant even in defeat, were volunteering no information until challenged with the facts.

From Melbourne, Colonel Jock Campbell, Lyon's partner in his earlier adventures, and now C.O. of the Services Reconnaissance Department, showered the search parties and interrogation teams with exhortations to find some clue to the fate of his companions. The P.O.W. camps, gaols, and detention centres were scoured, but no trace of the "Rimau" party could be found. They had disappeared utterly. Preliminary interrogation of the captured Japanese officers of the Seventh Area Army and the first search in their files produced nothing.

Then came the first break. A fortnight or so after the Allies had retaken Singapore, a tall, dignified young Malayan chieftain arrived by junk from the islands to the south. It was the valiant Amir Silalahi of Senajang, who had laboured so loyally three years earlier to help the fugitives from the Japanese invasion along Lyon's escape route through Sumatra to safety in Ceylon and India. Deposed by the Japanese, he had managed to survive the occupation and now came to seek out the former British administrators who had been his friends, if any were still alive.

He was soon made welcome. The Japanese garrison

and their Kempeitai gestapo were still terrorising his home islands in the Lingga Archipelago, but he had managed to escape and now sought British aid to drive them out. But he had an even more interesting story to tell. At the end of 1944, he reported, a group of British and Australian servicemen had been captured in the area of Temiang and had been held briefly in the cells of the police station at Singkep before being transferred to Singapore. Here was the first likely clue to the fate of Operation "Rimau."

In two naval launches a heavily armed party thrummed south to Singkep with the restored Amir Silalahi. There, in the police records, kept in Malay characters, they were able to check that nine "white men" had been received into custody at various dates towards the end of the previous December. Most of the names recorded were indecipherable, although one unmistakeably spelt out the word "Ingleton." On another grubby piece of paper, written in English block letters in three different hands, stood the names Captain Carey, Warrant Officer Warren, Able Seaman Marsh.

The interrogation teams fanned out amongst the islands, urged on by the possibility that some of the "Rimau" operatives might still be hiding out under the protection of friendly natives. In their leap-frog advance to the north in the final stages of the war, the Allied forces had often succeeded in rescuing "coast watchers," baled-out airmen, and the crews from sunken ships who had taken refuge in the jungles of the far-flung archipelagoes of the South Seas. With the tide of war turning and hatred of Japanese oppression reaching its height, hundreds of islanders had risked their lives to hide and feed the white men who sought their aid. Ivan Lyon's tough commandos, trained in survival tactics, might have fared better than most.

Within a fortnight there was no hope left. The pattern of disaster, laboriously assembled from the interrogation of Japanese prisoners and Malay islanders, was only too complete. Not a single "tiger" was left alive, although they had given a magnificent account of themselves. The last ten survivors had been executed by the sword, after a brief court-martial, barely three weeks before the end of the war in the Far East.

On leaving Pejantan, Lyon had altered his plans and sailed first for Merapas, to ensure that Carey and the stores were safe. Warrant Officer Warren and two of the Australian commandos were put ashore to join Carey, leaving only a minimum crew to man the junk under Otto Ingleton and carry the operatives to within Sleeping Beauty range of Singapore Roads. By this time Lyon had decided to scuttle the junk once the attack was launched and use the folboats for the return to base. With the party pared down to its minimum strength, it would even be possible to tow two or three empty folboats as spares.

Then, probably on October 6, *Mustika* weighed anchor and, sailing south about Bintang Island, plunged into the maze of islands of the Rhio Archipelago. It is only possible to guess at the course they followed, but the junk must have crossed the Rhio Strait, entered the "inland sea" either by the Dempu or Temiang Strait, and then sailed north-west up the Tjombol

Strait round Boelan Island. By the evening of October 10 they were off Kasoe Island, due south and little more than twelve miles from the island of Singapore. Another five miles would have found them at Pulau Subar, from which Lyon had launched his "Jaywick" attack. There was nothing but the Strait of Singapore itself left to cross in the Sleeping Beauties.

It was off Kasoe Island that the junk was sighted from an observation post on land manned by the Japanese-controlled native police. Perhaps a moment of carelessness brought too many members of the expedition on deck to look at their goal, but the sight of what looked like white men clearly aroused the suspicions of the alert look-outs, and four constables, with Inspector Ben Shiapel, put out in their motorboat to investigate.

What happened then there is no living survivor to describe. The "tigers" carried a formidable armament, a couple of rocket Piats, four Bren guns, tommy guns, and a full armoury of silent Stens, more than sufficient to sink a native patrol boat. Doubtless the silent Stens were used and to good effect. The patrol boat was riddled and sank with all its occupants dead.

It must have been a heart-breaking moment for Lyon. The expedition was intact within sight of its goal, but even though the immediate challenge had been beaten off, the alarm would soon be raised. Every aeroplane and naval craft in the Singapore area would be out searching for them. To press home the attack would have been folly and the Sleeping Beauty operatives would not have stood a chance. He took the only decision possible, ordered the folboats to be assembled and launched with sufficient supplies and then scuttled the junk with her precious cargo in deep water. A 500-pound charge of explosive had been fitted in the bilges for this purpose, but there is nothing in the Japanese records to suggest that this was fired, and the party must have opened *Mustika*'s sea-cocks.

The canoe flotilla was split into four parties under Lyon, Davidson, Page, and Ross, with orders to make their way separately back to Merapas, go to ground, and wait for the rescue submarine.

According to Japanese accounts, it was two days before a report of the attack reached the Singapore garrison. An immediate massive search was ordered and Japanese troops on all the islands were alerted to look for the fugitives.

Thereafter accounts of the pursuit are understandably confused, but it does seem as if all four canoe parties met by chance on Asore Island in the middle of the Rhio Straits about a week later. There the Japanese caught up with them. A major skirmish began on October 16 at three o'clock in the afternoon which lasted until half past nine the following morning. It was here that Lyon and Ross met their deaths, fighting a rear-guard action to enable the others to escape. The Japanese were halted, the patrol commander and at least one of his soldiers were killed, two more were wounded, and the rest withdrew, after capturing two folboats, which they brought back to Bintang Island.

Before leaving they made two fine graves with white crosses for Ivan Lyon and his brother officer.

That is the only pathetically brief note in the records concerning the manner of Lyon's end. It would be possible, with a little imagination, to concoct a vivid account of those last hours, but it would be fiction, and Lyon deserves better than that. His own reports and letters are so laconic and self-effacing, his tribute to his comrades-in-arms so consistently generous, that he would not have wished to be singled out as the sole hero of his expedition.

The fact remains that he was the unquestioned leader and organiser of his three fantastic wartime voyages—in the *Hin Lee* from Sumatra to Ceylon, in *Krait*, and then in *Mustika*. All are epics of war and it seems barely credible that they were inspired by the same man. It is fascinating to see how a man's character remains constant, yet develops and leaves its mark. He is recognisably the same person sailing his schoolboy canoe across the North Sea to Denmark and leading his selected cut-throats to Singapore. Restless, unwilling to conform to the tidy, neutral habits of the world around him, he probably found fulfilment only in the alarums of irregular warfare. He would have met his death in action sooner or later. One of the last remarks he made to his sister before leaving England concerned his plans once the Allies had won. "I shall travel round the world, looking for other wars to fight," he told her. The end had come too soon. His last act had been to give his men a chance to get away. His Highland ancestors would have approved.

His self-sacrifice brought them only brief respite. The Japanese were not going to let them escape now. Harried from island to island, they were given no rest.

"In October 1944 I saw three white men on the island of Pankil," Raja Mun, a native of Penengad Island, told the search teams. "They called to me and told me not to be afraid. They asked me for food and said they were Australians and also told me they had reached Pankil with two canoes. I did not see the canoes. The Australians were dressed in green and had two Bren guns and three pistols. One was a very tall man and had a red cord on his shoulder. They were not wearing any badges.

"After I left them I went to Tandjoengpinang and reported what I had seen to Tuan Namahit, who at that time was district officer for the Japanese on Bintang Island. Namahit gave me 20 dollars and took me to the Japanese headquarters. I told the Japanese what I had seen and they asked me to lead them back to where I had left the Australians. I agreed to do this and they gave Namahit 50 dollars which he gave to me. I then went with the Japanese to Pankil but we could not find the Australians.

"They then took me to Asore and Tapai. At Tapai I was shown the bodies of two white men and was asked to identify them as two of the men I spoke to at Pankil. I told the Japanese they were two of the party, though the bodies I was shown were not the same as the men I saw at Pankil. I was afraid of the Japanese, so told them they were two of the party I saw at Pankil. I went to the Japanese in the first place because

I was afraid if I did not tell them and they found out, I would be killed and my house burnt."

It must be assumed that one of the two dead men was Davidson, as his name never appears again. This was another serious loss. Only Davidson rivalled Lyon as a jungle fighter and navigator. His knowledge of the islands, fierce leadership, and ingenuity might well have prolonged their survival for months. He must have sacrificed himself like Lyon to cover the escape of his companions.

The sand rake which was his hallmark was doubtless picked up by one of the other members of the expedition and taken on to Merapas, which the remaining survivors reached before the end of the month, holing up at their food cache under the command of Page. They remained undetected until November 4, only four days before the first rendez-vous date with *Tantalus*. Then, tragically, the Japanese caught up with them again and destroyed all hopes of rescue. Abdul Wahad, the head man of nearby Mapor Island in the Rhio group, was a witness of the final heartbreak:

"A motorboat containing about 17 Japanese came to my island and inquired if any Europeans had been seen. I said I knew nothing. The Japanese threatened me and forced me to go with them to Merapas by motorboat. At the south-west corner we sighted a Malay fisherman. They questioned him and when he said there were no whites there they beat him. He repeated there were no whites on the island. About noon the Japanese went into the jungle and I heard the sound of heavy firing. About four o'clock they returned to the shore and brought with them the Japanese commander dead and a wounded Japanese soldier. The soldier was wounded in the head. They forced the fisherman and his wife to carry the dead body out of the jungle and beat them as they carried it.

"I heard the Japanese say they had killed one European but I did not see the body. The motorboat was despatched with one Japanese to Kijang to report the death of the Japanese captain. The remainder stayed the night in a house near the shore. About eight or nine at night several motorboats arrived with at least a hundred men and they started to patrol both on land and by sea and forced all fishing boats to go ashore. One motorboat was sent back to Kijang the same night with the dead body of the captain.

"Next day I saw that a number of strange articles had been loaded into one of the motorboats: what looked like tins of petrol, round bundles in sacking, a small wireless set, and one soft green hat. About eight in the morning the motorboats left for Kijang and I was taken away, but a large number of Japanese remained on the island.

"The fisherman and his wife were brought back at the same time. They were very badly beaten and were detained at Kijang for about 20 days. The woman was four months pregnant and she had a miscarriage.

"I escaped from the Japanese as soon as we reached Kijang and returned to Mapor. There were no natives left on Merapas. I heard that Japanese garrison was kept on Merapas for about four months, but I did not hear of any further Europeans being found there."

The clues found by Chapman and Croton now fell into a pattern. *Mustika* had called first at Merapas, most of the party had reached the rendez-vous, but had been flushed out by the Japanese, who removed their stores. There is no further confirmation of a "Rimau" casualty on Merapas. As far as is known, the remaining survivors got away in their folboats to the south. Fortunately for Walter Chapman and *Tantalus,* the Japanese garrison had called off their watch at the pick-up island too soon.

Abdul Wahad was a brave and loyal man, but either his memory for dates or the rest of his evidence was faulty, as he went on to tell the interrogators: "About four months ago [this would have meant mid-June 1945] Dollah, a fisherman, came to me at Mapor and told me that while he was fishing off Sentut Island, north-east of Mapor, his anchor broke loose and he went ashore to get a stone to replace it. While he was ashore five men wearing European clothes came out of the jungle and asked him for fish. He gave them what he had. He told me that he was very frightened, as he believed the island to be uninhabited and three of the five had black faces. They were not as far as he could tell Asiatics. They offered him cigarettes but he was afraid to take them.

"As soon as he had given them the fish he left hurriedly and came to report what he had seen to me. There were Japanese on Mapor Island at the time. I ordered him not to tell anyone else what he had seen. I had previously given orders to my people that if any of them saw any Europeans they were to come and tell me but they were not to tell the Japanese. Dollah went home and kept his secret."

This information sent the interrogation teams racing for Sentut, which they found deserted and without even a water supply. On the beach there was a small tube of Bostick solution, used for repairing the folboats, and the remains of an old fire near the water's edge.

Hunted, their supplies running low again, the surviving "tigers" had pushed on south to Temiang and the Lingga Archipelago. Japanese troops and the brutal Kempeitai military police were terrorising the natives in all the villages, ordering them on pain of death to give no shelter to the fugitives and report all information. Six more commandos lost their lives on the way in skirmishes, but the remainder struggled on. For most of them the end came on the three islands of Selear, Boeia, and Sepangka. Between December 18 and 28 ten of them were captured and brought to the cells in the police station at Singkep. They were Ingleton, Page, Carey, Warren, Stewart, Fletcher, Gooley, Hardy, Falls, and Biffo Marsh, the joker of "Jaywick," who was badly wounded in the shoulder. Shortly after the prisoners had been transferred to Singapore at the beginning of January, he died.

Three more had escaped the net—Sargent, the incredibly tough Australian infantry subaltern, and two others, whose names have gone unrecorded. Incredibly, they reached the little island of Romang, south-east of Timor. The mind boggles at the feat of endurance this represents. They had paddled nearly 2000 miles and might have reached Darwin or New Guinea and safety if they had not been intercepted. Off Romang, Sargent's canoe stranded on some fishing stakes. One of his companions was taken by a shark, the other killed, and Sargent captured and brought back to Singapore.

The ten survivors were held for a time by the Japanese water police, where there is every reason to suppose they were decently treated. In March 1945 they were handed over to the Judicial Department of the Seventh Army Area and lodged in Outram Road gaol. This was the Japanese military prison, maintained principally for the punishment of their own personnel. There were a few Allied prisoners, either persistent escapees or others facing charges of sabotage or other severe offences.

The captured "tigers" were housed in separate cells in an upper gallery, sealed away from any compatriots, although it transpired subsequently that they had been able to pass the occasional whispered message describing their identity. Very few of the Allied prisoners left Outram Road alive to tell the tale. The "Rimau" men were never recorded as normal prisoners of war, but their fantastic exploit had so impressed and overawed their captors, and their personal attitude of defiance so appealed to these exponents of the Bushido and Samurai tradition, that they were treated with great respect, decently fed, and supplied with books, chocolates, and cigarettes. Their chief benefactor was the interpreter assigned to them, Furuta, whose conduct, and their recorded appreciation of it, earned him his freedom when he was subsequently captured by the Allies.

The Japanese High Command was less generous. In due course the ten men were brought to trial at Raffles College on charges of "perfidy and espionage." The chief allegations were that the "Rimau" party had not worn proper military uniform, that they had operated the junk under the Japanese flag, and that the members of the expedition had been engaged in military espionage in enemy territory.

Furuta, who cooperated willingly with the Allied interrogation teams, was challenged about the "perfidy" charge, and reminded that during the invasion of Malaya in 1941 the Japanese had come over the border in Malay and Chinese dress.

"I am astonished to hear it," Furuta replied. "I wish I had known it at the time; I might have been able to help them in their defence. They were heroes, and I tried hard to help them, by speaking to many people, some of them big people. I even dreamed of trying to help them to get away from the Water Police, where they were well treated and lightly guarded. I dreamed of helping them to get to Changi, where they might have been hidden away by the prisoners-of-war. They were heroes, sir; even the Court was reluctant to condemn them and said that they were heroes."

They were tried under Japanese military law. The charges, in the quaint translation made later for the Allied interrogation teams, read: "The clothing worn by the members of the "Rimau" project were green coloured shirts and trousers and also beret caps of the same colour, but except for a few commisssoned officers, the members from their date of departure willingly refrained from wearing badges to show their ranks, also refrained from using caps and so their appearance was such that it was difficult to recognise them as regular fighting members of either British or Australian forces.

"Furthermore, since the day of departure from Pejantan Island, all members applied on them so-called commando or demouflage dyeing stuff and dyed into brown the exposed part of their skins such as face, arms and legs. In addition to that, Lieutenant-Colonel Lyon, Captain Page, the accused person, and six more members were wearing loin cloth called *sarong*, the one used by the native Malayans and continued their voyage on the junk without taking off the Japanese national flag, which had been hoisted on the stern of the junk by the Malayan crews, and whenever the junk was sighted by the Japanese patrol plane or crafts, they displayed another Japanese national flag, which they had prepared beforehand, and pretended as if the junk was an ordinary civilian vessel, crewed by native inhabitants, who were peacefully engaged in daily works under Japanese military administration, and with those deceptive activities they succeeded in passing the guarded area and infiltrated into the outlying area of the port of Singapore.

"While acting as above, they contrived to collect information to be reported to their home country, and designed the accused Ingleton for sketching, the accused Page for photographing and Lieutenant-Commander Davidson for documentary recording. These three persons reconnoitred in their disguise clothing the conditions of guards of islands south of Singapore, state of administration of ships in those areas, trend of public mind there, strength of Japanese navy crafts operating in Rhio Straits, conditions of bauxite being dug out in Lingga Island etc. and made sketching records of our fleet in Rhio Straits and bauxite mines, also photographed the same and engaged in collection and recording of the military information. Other accused persons, also in their disguised costumes, exerted to collect information for the purpose.

"Furthermore the accused Carey, while on Merapas Island, made very detailed record of the strength of our fleet operating near the base and of movements of our aircrafts over the area, and recorded the same in his notebook. In this way they were engaged secretly and without due qualifications in collections of military information within our operational area."

It was suggested to the prisoners before their trial that if they adopted a humble attitude and pleaded for mercy they might get away with their lives. The suggestion was contemptuously dismissed and the "tigers" remained defiant to the last. As the senior surviving officer, Otto Ingleton is surely entitled to a major share of the credit for maintaining their magnificent morale.

The Japanese, by what methods we have no means of telling, had obtained a clear idea of the details of the expedition. *Porpoise*, *Mustika*, Pejantan, Merapas, the Sleeping Beauties, all figure in the transcript of the trial, but nowhere is there the faintest reference to "Jaywick" and *Krait*. Marsh, before he died, Page, and Falls must have been under an intolerable strain during the long months of captivity, but not a whisper escaped them. It seems inconceivable that the Japanese should not have connected the two raids, and in the six months before the trial the subject must have come up frequently in interrogation. Perhaps, having warded off the "Rimau" raid, they were prepared, for once, to treat their prisoners with respect. They certainly obtained little satisfaction from them in Court.

"What is this jungle-green uniform?" the judges wanted to know. "It is the uniform of the Australian Army in the tropics," the prisoners answered. Falls had his own explanation: "I am a navy man and therefore do not wear badges of rank," he told them tersely.

Page, the leader of the skirmish on Merapas, was asked: "Did you yourself kill any Japanese soldiers?" He answered proudly: "I am an officer of the British Army and I know that my aim was good."

Even the tortured reasoning of the prosecutor, Major Kamiya, in his closing address, could not conceal the respect which these doomed men inspired in their captors: "With such fine determination they infiltrated into the Japanese area," Kamiya proclaimed to the Court. "We do not hesitate to call them the real heroes of a forlorn hope. It has been fortunate for us that their intention was frustrated halfway, but when we fathom their intention and share their feelings we cannot but spare a tear for them. The valorous spirit of these men reminds us of the daring enterprise of our heroes of the Naval Special Attack Corps who died in May 1942 in their attack on Sydney Harbour.

"The same admiration and respect that the Australian Government, headed by the Premier and all the Australian people, showed to those heroes of ours we must return to these heroes in our presence. When the deed is so heroic, its sublime spirit must be respected, and its success or failure becomes a secondary matter.

"These heroes must have left Australia with sublime patriotism flaming in their breasts, and with the confident expectation of all the Australian people on their shoulders. The last moment of a hero must be historic and it must be dramatic. Heroes have more regard for their reputation than for anything else. As we respect them, so we feel our duty of glorifying their last moments as they deserve: and by our doing so the names of these heroes will remain in the hearts of the British and Australian people for evermore.

"In the circumstances I consider that a death sentence should be given to each of the accused."

According to the summary of the proceedings in the Japanese files, Major Ingleton then stood up and thanked the Court for referring to them as patriotic heroes. All ten men were sentenced to death. The date on the court record is July 5, 1945. Two days later sentence was carried out.

The rest of their story is better told in the words of the records of the Judiciary Department of the

Japanese Seventh Area Army and of eye-witnesses of their last days together:

"After the trial all the members of the party were given extra rations and, in accordance with their request, were kept together in one room so that they could freely converse with one another. Their attitude was really admirable. They were always clear and bright, and not a single shadow of dismal or melancholy mood did they show. All who saw them were profoundly impressed."

At Outram Road gaol, their warders included four Korean "trusties," themselves under long prison sentence for offences against the Japanese military code. One of these, named Noh Bok Kun, who had been told that the ten were captured airmen, remembered clearly: "Their heads were cropped, all were young, and they had slight beards. For three days before their execution they were given good food, milk, and tobacco. They all knew they were going to be executed. When they left their cell to enter the two trucks which were to take them to their execution they appeared in high spirits, laughing and talking and shaking hands with one another. All of us prisoners were amazed."

At ten o'clock in the morning of July 7, the grim little convoy arrived at the execution ground, a desolate stretch of country near Reformatory Road, covered with sparse scrub and the insect-eating plants called Dutchman's-pipe. It had seen the last moments of hundreds of Japanese prisoners. Yet somehow the light-hearted courage of these latest victims touched some chord in the brutalised heart of the officer in charge: "They were all given cigarettes and rested," he reported. "Then, in accordance with their request, they were allowed to shake hands with one another. They all stood up, shook hands merrily and even laughingly in a very harmonious manner, and bade each other farewell. The sky was clear and the scenery was beautiful.

"Major Ingleton on behalf of the whole party requested that the commandant of the prison and the prosecuting officer should tell the Japanese interpreter that they were all most grateful for the courtesy and kindness which he had shown them for a long time past. He said again that they must not forget to give the interpreter this message. All who heard him were deeply moved.

"The execution started and it was over by noon. Every member of the party went to his death calmly and composedly, and there was not a single person there who was not inspired by their fine attitude."

Alone among the many graves on this execution heath, their last resting places were marked with ten rough wooden crosses.

In his report to the Seventh Area Army Commander, even Major-General Ohtsuka, head of the Judiciary Department which had sent so many people to their deaths, felt obliged to pay one last tribute. The summarised transcript quotes him as commenting "on the patriotism, fearless enterprise, heroic behaviour, and sublime end of all members of this party, praising them as the flower of chivalry, which should be taken as a model by the Japanese. He concluded by saying that all Japanese soldiers should be inspired by their fine attitude and on reflection must feel the necessity of bracing up their own spirits in emulation if they hoped to win the war."

Three weeks later the Allied atom bombs fell on Hiroshima and Nagasaki.

POSTSCRIPT

IVAN LYON'S FAMILY WAS LEFT LONG IN DOUBT AS TO his fate. He was first posted missing in May 1945, and it was not until January 1946, after the exhaustive enquiries in Singapore, that his death was officially presumed. In due course, his body was exhumed from Asore Island and reburied in Kranji war cemetery on Singapore Island. The family has placed a memorial plaque on the outside wall of St. George's Garrison Church at Tanglin.

Mrs. Gabrielle Lyon survived the war in Japanese internment, but when she was repatriated to Australia with her five-year-old son she found that not only her husband but her mother and father were dead. She returned to England for her first meeting with the Lyon family, and her son, Clive, has since passed through his father's old school, Harrow.

It was not until August 1, 1946, that public reference was first made to the two expeditions Ivan Lyon had led into the heart of Japanese territory. On that day Mr. Forde, the Australian Minister for the Army, made the following statement in the House of Representatives:

"The story of a well kept secret has now been released with the publication of the awards for gallantry to a small but determined band of officers and men who carried the war thousands of miles behind the Japanese lines during the days of 1943, when Japan was flushed with the fortunes of conquest. The exploit was a joint effort by a party of fourteen comprising ten Australians and four members of the British forces. Unfortunately six members of this party lost their lives in a subsequent operation in 1944. The awards were approved by the King in 1944 but details were withheld for security reasons. I give now the names and awards and also the home state of the Australians:

British Army. Captain (later Lieutenant-Colonel) I. Lyon, M.B.E., Gordon Highlanders, D.S.O.

Royal Navy. Lieutenant (later Lieutenant-Commander) D. N. Davidson, R.N.V.R., D.S.O.

New South Wales. Lieutenant (later Captain) R. C. Page, A.I.F., D.S.O.

(Lives of above lost in subsequent operation in 1944.)

Queensland. Corporal A. Crilly, A.I.F., Military Medal.

British Army. Corporal R. G. Morris, R.A.M.C., Military Medal.

Royal Navy. Leading Stoker J. P. McDowell, R.N., D.S.M.

New South Wales. Able Seaman W. C. Falls, R.A.N. (life lost in subsequent operation in 1944), D.S.M.

Western Australia. Acting Able Seaman A. W. Jones, R.A.N., D.S.M.

Queensland. Able Seaman A. W. Huston, R.A.N. (life lost in subsequent operation in 1944), D.S.M.

New South Wales. Lieutenant H. C. Carse, R.A.N.V.R., Mention in Despatches.

Queensland. Acting Leading Seaman K. P. Cain, R.A.N., Mention in Despatches.

New South Wales. Leading Telegraphist H. S. Young, R.A.N., Mention in Despatches.

Queensland. Able Seaman F. W. Marsh, R.A.N. (life lost in subsequent operation in 1944), Mention in Despatches.

South Australia. Acting Able Seaman M. Berryman, R.A.N., Mention in Despatches.

"The citation of the awards mentions 'outstanding bravery and devotion to duty under circumstances of extreme hazard.' This party after thorough and arduous training in Australia, undertook the hazardous journey of 2,000 miles unescorted through enemy-patrolled waters to Singapore. Despite a number of narrow escapes from detection the party continued with great determination and after keeping Singapore harbour under secret observation for several days, made a silent attack on the night of 26th September 1943, selecting this night on account of the suitable concentration of shipping. Despite the hazard of entering a closely guarded and patrolled harbour in enemy hands, the party pressed home their attack and withdrew without loss. This attack resulted in the loss by the Japanese, through sinking and burning, of seven ships of the tanker and freighter class, totalling 37,000 tons, at a time when its shipping was hard pressed to support its armed forces. The members of the party were then faced with the 2,000 mile return journey in constant danger of detection, which they well knew meant certain death.

"They reached Australia without loss or mishap on 19th October 1943 having spent over forty days in enemy occupied and controlled areas under conditions of constant strain and danger and having carried out a highly successful and crippling attack on the enemy, concerning the method of which the Japanese are still in the dark. I am sure that all Honourable Members will join with me in expressing admiration of the heroic deeds of these gallant men. Our hearts go out in sympathy to the relatives of those who subsequently lost their lives. It was by such deeds that the Allies won the war."

On November 6, 1949, a memorial to the members of the Services Reconnaissance Department who had lost their lives during the war was unveiled at Careening Bay Camp, Garden Island, off Fremantle, where the members of Operation "Rimau" trained. Blue-grey Western Australian granite blocks frame the red-polished granite face stones which record the names of Ivan Lyon and his party and the 112 other gallant men who died on sabotage raids and "coast watching" duties during the Pacific campaign.

Lyon, Davidson, Page, and the three seamen, Falls, Huston, and Marsh, had already left on Operation "Rimau" when their awards were approved and never learnt of them. For security reasons, the citations had not been gazetted, and *The Times* list of casualties published on January 23, 1946, only attributed to Lyon the M.B.E. he had received for his work at the fall of Singapore.

The citation for the D.S.O. awarded for Operation "Jaywick" reads: "Major Lyon was responsible for the planning and personnel command of operations against the enemy which were carried out in most hazardous conditions with the greatest gallantry and determination. Major Lyon's coolness and resourcefulness in the face of the enemy, and the example of confidence and disregard for personal safety set by him in his leadership of the party were the main factors in the complete success of the expedition."

The stringent regulations governing the award of posthumous decorations have prevented the recognition of those who took part in Operation "Rimau." Only the Victoria Cross, the George Cross, or a Mention in Despatches may be awarded posthumously, and the details of the qualifying deed must be attested by at least two independent witnesses. It is an additional tragedy that no one should be left alive to testify to the quality of Lyon's leadership and sacrifice and to the magnificent manner in which Ingleton maintained the morale of the survivors of the expedition captured by the Japanese. Perhaps now that the full story of their extraordinary exploit has finally been pieced together, it can serve as their memorial.

MALAYA
STRAIT OF MALACCA
SUMATRA
Natuna Is.
Anambas Is.
Sth. Natuna Is.
Tg. Da
1 Maru 2 E.V.
Tioman Is.
Aor I.
5th. Nov.
AREA
PROHIBITED
19th. Nov.
21st. Nov.
Singapore
RHIO Arch.
MERAPAS Is.
LINGGA Arch.
Tambelan Is.
Singkawa
3 Marus 2 E.V.
Pejantan Is.
27th. Oct
Pontiana
Karimata Arch.
Padang
BANGKA Is.
Djambi
Karimata Strait
Gaspar Str.
Palembang
BILLITON Is.
26th. Oct.
24th Nov.
Benkoelen
INDIAN
OCEAN
Teloekbetoeng
Duitzend Is.
Sunda Str.
Batavia
(Djakarta)
Bandoeng
26th.
Bata
Tjilatja
J
J A
Swamp
Land over 3,000 ft.
1,000 to 3,000 ft.
RIMAU PICK UP SORTIE
TRACK CHART OF H.M.SUBMARINE TANTALUS
Miles
0 50 100 150 200 250 300